MOSTLY WOMEN

MOSTLY WOMEN

A Photographer's Life

MICHAEL WARD

Granta Books
London

Granta Publications, 2/3 Hanover Yard, Noel Road, London N1 8BE

First published in Great Britain by Granta Books 2006

A CIP catalogue record for this book is available
from the British Library.

1 3 5 7 9 10 8 6 4 2

ISBN-13: 978-1-86207-849-9
ISBN-10: 1-86207-849-1

Typeset by M Rules
Printed and bound in Great Britain by The Cromwell Press

Acknowledgements

My fond gratitude to a motley cast in order of appearance –

Cal McCrystal – a colleague at the *Sunday Times*, who to my surprise suggested an autobiography in which to put my pictures. Elizabeth, my wife – whose gallant and unceasing support I can only interpret as love. Harry Evans – who when first shown the beginnings of this book, was astonishingly encouraging. Maggie Angeloglou – who applied her professional expertise with great understanding to the manuscript. Roger Schlesinger – whose opinion that the book was highly publishable, spurred me on. Mark Holborn of Jonathan Cape – who suggested showing the manuscript to Granta. Kathleen Herron – deputy managing editor of the *Sunday Times* who so graciously authorized the use of my photographs. Michael Chapman – a neighbouring computer expert – who considered me 'a non-trivial user', nevertheless helped me through so many potentially disastrous moments. Chay Catt – who took over my computing problems providing valuable advice about hard disk and memory problems. At Granta: Ian Jack – an old colleague at the *Sunday Times* – whose edit was nothing less than miraculous; Gail Lynch, publisher, for her unflinching support; Sarah Wasley who was imperturbably optimistic about any problems I feared might occur; Sajidah Ahmad – who was irresistibly and attentively helpful at the copy-editing stage; and Louise Campbell whose promotional zeal filled me with nervous apprehension, yet confidence. And finally Terence Pepper – Curator Of Photographs Of The National Portrait Gallery – who not only kindly mounted an exhibition to launch this book, but to whom I owe a great debt for including me in his advancement of the appreciation of photography in this country over the last few decades. Of course there are many others who have, by their interest, kept alive my hopes of finishing this book and I thank them very much.

To my wife, Elizabeth

Foreword

Michael Ward's book makes me want to kick myself. There he was at the *Sunday Times*, when I was editor, coming in from riots and garden parties, theatre dressing rooms and party conferences, and never once did it occur to me that he had two sets of eyes: one for selecting the news image and another for social commentary. Editors always assume that photographers have an antipathy for words, and it is not an unreasonable assumption, given how painful it seems to be for them to confide anything beyond the barest identification of the subject and sometimes not even that. I've always admired how Lord Northcliffe coped one night on his *Daily Mail*. Told that nobody knew anything about the photograph of a young woman lying around, not even her name, he seized it for the front page and slapped on the headline 'Who is she?'

I don't recall Michael being any more forthcoming with words than any other photographer, but I do recall him being a lot of fun. He always had about him the air of the man about town — after all, he was married to a dancing star and wore smart black leather jackets and rode a flamboyant motorcycle. As one photographer in a talented group, he was ready to tackle anything, but I thought he was at his best coaxing actors — his father, Ronald, had been a success in the West End — and he was always alert for the off-beat and the comic. He wasn't even set up to shoot when I held a lunch at the Garrick Club on behalf of the Photographers' Gallery and the guest of honour, Chancellor Denis Healey, made a joke that convulsed the room. None of us afterwards could remember why we were laughing so hard, but somehow in that nanosecond Michael caught the moment of spontaneous combustion, though he didn't realize it until he got back to the office.

Such photographic dexterity we took for granted. We would have had a brighter paper if we had been aware of Michael's hidden talent for the telling vignette and fleshed out our news pictures with his reflections and diary fragments – adventures on the way to the darkroom. That is the simple structure of this captivating book. It is a random compilation of photograph and memory. There is no overarching theme, no derring-do, no adumbrations on the morals of the age, no didactics on photojournalism. It wanders, like good gossip, and it is all the more enjoyable for that. One minute Michael is in the headmaster's study at Eton, getting dressed down for talking to the boys about fagging, another in Knightsbridge at the scene of the Iranian embassy siege, another lingering in the fleshpots of Soho; and then again he revisits the poignancy of a family death and some of the collisions in his serial marriages. 'I reached a new low in my behaviour today. I spat at Elizabeth. I was ashamed – it put me in a sort of shocked state. I was trying not to be violent to her and, on the instant, thought it wouldn't hurt her but would relieve my frustration.' He is talking about his fifth wife, the beautiful acting, dancing and singing star Elizabeth Seal (winner of a Tony for her lead in *Irma La Douce*), and looking at his picture of her sitting pensively in tights in a dance studio, one wonders, 'How could he? How could he?' To me, and I think all his colleagues on the paper, Michael saw it as a mission in life to cheer up everyone around him. He didn't seem to smoulder as a day's work was selected or rejected. There is a perfect representation of that agreeable Michael Ward in the picture by Sally Soames on the night the *Sunday Times* resumed publication in 1980 after an absence of a year. He expresses the exhilaration everyone felt when the first edition was delivered to the newsroom: the freshly inked paper held up with a flourish, big grin, cig in mouth, George Robey eyebrows raised in exuberance.

It was this Michael Ward, the confidence-builder, who came with me when, with great misgivings, I went along to the BM showrooms on Park Lane to buy a big motorcycle: rashly I had admired his bike and romanticized my university days on a Triumph 250. I hadn't ridden a motorcycle in twenty years. Somehow, with Michael as sweeper, I wobbled home to Highgate. Not long afterwards, Michael used his charm to get us both attached to a police training squad for a speedy run from London to Salisbury Plain. We swept through the West Country for hours, disguised as patrolmen. We did not dare to lay our bikes over as perilously as the squad but gratifyingly we had the same effect on motorists, who slowed to a crawl as we roared up. Yes, and I have a Michael

Ward action photo to prove it.

Perhaps Michael's greatest gift in surfing through life is that he does not take himself too seriously. He could impress us with the piano scholarship he won to Trinity College of Music, when he was fifteen, but he says he was unemployable as a musician; he could elaborate on his acting roles in movies and rep, but he says he couldn't remember his lines so he gave up acting for bartending and running errands on movie sets. He got into photography persuading racing star Stirling Moss to have his picture taken — and then had to borrow Moss's Rolleiflex because he had no camera of his own. Michael's lack of pretence is not artifice and it is the source of the effervescence in his book.

Harold Evans
New York, 2006

Part One

1

The most convincing way to persuade people that one is knowledgeable about photography, or perhaps any craft, is to tell them airily that one knows nothing. Often this is modesty so false that the vanity behind it comes shining through. In my case, the statement is nearly true. I started to take pictures for money in 1958, when I was twenty-nine years old. A late start, but in the years that followed I made up for it; putting together this book, I had to search through the work of 5,500 assignments for magazines and newspapers, chiefly the *Sunday Times*. And yet almost fifty years later, after a lifetime with a camera, I know as much or as little about the processes of photography as a decent amateur. I can use cameras, given time, and I can print from black and white negatives, but I do both without really knowing what I am doing. I have little technical or optical knowledge and even less chemical. As for the aesthetics of the photograph, or what you might call the sensibilities of the photographer, I am by no means sure what separates the great from the good, or the good from the indifferent. Many of the shots I took were adequate to their purpose: to illustrate their accompanying story. Others were good, I think, as portraits in their own right. Looking through them, I still can't be certain how many have a magic of their own, something extra in them that gives you another reason to look at them. I have had pictures published in anthologies and shown in a few respectable exhibitions, but I never became a famous photographer (of whom, to me, there have always seemed a great many).

What is it that makes a picture – a documentary photograph – worth looking at? Its technical excellence? The particularity of its subject? Does it help if it documents a historical era or a memorable event? Does it help if its subject is

3

famous? Does its worth depend on the fame or distinction of the periodical in which it first appeared? The answer to these questions is yes – sometimes. But to my mind, there is also room in the world for pictures of nowhere in particular and of nothing in particular, taken by nobody in particular. I remember an exhibition at the Museum of Modern Art in New York which gathered together the snaps of unknown families in unknown places by unknown photographers. Each one was worth looking at, each one revealed something. Photography is the most democratic and chancy of arts: everything depends on what is in the frame for the fraction of the second when the shutter is opened. In this way, if in no other, I hope there may be a few of my pictures worth saving from the mass I took while trying to earn my living as a photographer.

I sometimes wonder if I should ever have been one at all, which at the age of seventy-seven is rather a useless speculation. I wanted to be a pianist. For a time, I was quite a bad actor. My father was an actor and my mother a dancer, and the business of performing to an audience was part of both their families' tradition. As a photographer, I think this inheritance may have helped me when I came to take pictures of people; the camera alone is a most unengaging thing, terrifying to some of its subjects, and I suppose my performance behind it helped people to relax in the same way a charming dentist might. But when I was a child, or so I now see, my parents' profession was far from a help to me. The self-absorption of my mother and father made them quite spectacularly careless; I grew up in a world of parental absences. My father, Ronnie, and my mother, Peggy, had been married three years when I came along and were to stay married for only another one. They were both good-looking – in my mother's case, beautiful – and they had their careers and they had their lovers. Their lives were full of opportunity and promise, sexual and romantic as well as professional. They were born to perform.

The earliest story I heard about my father's family was the death scene of my great-grandfather Theophilus Frederick Ward in 1875. His seven children were gathered round his bed watching him slowly expire, when, with a great effort, he leaned forward, beckoned them to come closer and very softly said, 'Can you all keep a secret?' They waited for their father to tell them what they hoped would be some news of inheritance, or at least a piece of family scandal, but after a long silence he said, 'So can I,' and died.

Secrets are those parts of our lives which we keep to ourselves for reasons of shame or practicality. To begin with, when we are young, we share them with nobody – but as we get older and become more able to understand them, we tend to start sharing them with others, sometimes to relieve our anxieties, sometimes to celebrate achievements in our lives. But right from the start these little-understood influences, which we sometimes turn into secrets, have been at work dividing our lives in two. Perhaps this is what André Gide meant when he talked about 'being' and 'appearing'. 'One must be to appear,' he wrote. We have a very private life and a life we are prepared to exhibit. The former perhaps influences the latter more than we would sometimes care to know. When I write this, I think of my five marriages and my mother and our long-kept and shaming secret, but all of us have such things in our lives, usually in a milder form. We are all so different behind our own front doors.

2

The earliest family photograph I have, taken probably in 1868, shows my grandfather, Robert Theophilus Ward with his brothers and sister.

My grandfather Theo was a fine, handsome man with a fashionable moustache, which he kept all his life. His first job was working for his mother, my great-grandmother, who was widowed with seven children and ran the Seven Stars pub in Carey Street, near the Law Courts in London. At fifteen he began piano lessons and three years later he was studying at the Royal Academy of Music, where he won bronze and silver medals for his piano playing. My father

From left, George Albert Ward, 10, Louisa Ward, 10, John Henry Ward, 6, and my grandfather Theophilus Ward, 5.

My grandfather Theo Ward with baby
Dudley, 1897.

My grandmother Marie Elizabeth Ward
with my father, Ronnie, and my Uncle
Dudley, 1902.

told me that Franz Liszt visited the Royal Academy towards the end of his life
and heard Theo play his Liebesträume No. 3. Liszt complimented him by
saying, 'I wish I could play it like that.' (Or so my father said – he was a great
romancer.) In 1889, while he was organist of Emmanuel Church, Dulwich,
Theo was asked to be musical director of Sir Charles Wyndham's Criterion
Theatre in Piccadilly Circus. In 1893 he went to Calcutta, where he wrote
music and conducted productions for a Mrs Brown-Potter and returned after
a year with a beautiful silver and ivory baton. In 1895 he married Marie
Elizabeth Rosa, the twenty-two-year-old daughter of a house painter, and in
1897 a son, my Uncle Dudley, was born. In 1898 he wrote and conducted the
ballets at the Winter Gardens, Blackpool, and in 1899 inaugurated the munic-
ipal orchestra in Eastbourne. There, in 1901 in a Victorian villa, my father was
born. A third son, Mackenzie, followed in 1904.

One day, Theo came home from an afternoon with his baton on
Eastbourne's bandstand to find his Steinway piano standing alone in the front

room. His wife, Marie Elizabeth, had sold the rest of the furniture for gin. She was an alcoholic. Nobody ever knew if it came from the strain of coping with three boys on a musician's salary, or was a sickness it was hopeless to fight.

Theo's personality endeared him to his orchestra and the people of Eastbourne. He composed works for the piano, songs, operettas, even an opera. He gave piano recitals and band concerts on the beach bandstand and more serious concerts in the Duke of Devonshire's Theatre. Then, in 1907, Eastbourne town council decided it needed to save money and insisted that the number of Theo's musicians be cut. Despite a public outcry, Theo resigned and was given a public testimonial, at which the mayor said that 'the name of Theo Ward would ever be remembered as the founder of high class public music in Eastbourne'.

This cartoon appeared in the *Eastbourne Gazette* when the council's intention to cut the players in the orchestra was announced:

The drawing indicates a low tide. In fact, Eastbourne was probably the high-water mark in my grandfather's career and his leaving of it the beginning of his disillusionment with life. He continued to live in a way that would persuade people that he was a successful gentleman musician, deploying his charm to outwit tradesmen and their unpaid bills, and he had some success. In 1909, he went to Paris to conduct *Peter Pan* at the Théâtre du Vaudeville, and the next year he was appointed musical director of the Garden's Company Orchestra in Buxton. But his private life was a mess. In 1912 he and Marie Elizabeth had another child, their only daughter, Beryl, but by then they led largely separate lives. Theo earned money away from home and his wife drank it. For a time, she lived with the children at 21 Oppidans Road in Primrose Hill with her uncle W. Weekes, known as 'Piggy' Weekes, who had sculpted one of the corners of the Albert Memorial. And then, in November 1914, Weekes died (to cover the mortgage and funeral expenses the solicitors sold a few paintings hanging in the hall – by Whistler, according to my father) and she and the children moved to 25 St James's Square, Holland Park.

The First World War was a few months old. Theo was on tour with a musical play. His eldest son, Dudley, was working at the Kolynos toothpaste factory and had moved to a rented room to avoid the chaos at home. And so it fell to my thirteen-year-old father to help with the running of the household, which included looking after Mack, now ten, and baby Beryl, now two. Ronnie wrote to his father in the desperate hope that he might be able to help. But it was Ronnie who had to help, until Theo died in 1935.

To: Theo Ward Esq.,	From: 21, Oppidans Road,
Musical Director of 'Europe,'	Primrose Hill,
Empire,	NW.
Nottingham.	Dec 10th 1914

Dear Dad,

    I am writing to you for Mother, as she says that she has not had time to write yet. She has now gone off to the dealers, down Piccadilly or somewhere, and I suppose that she will not come untill [*sic*] late tonight, which is generally the way now. Of course she has a lot to see after, but does not go about it in the proper way, she will not take any notice of what the solicitor advises her, she will have her own way, and says she will not dispose the house and wants to keep it on for us. Of course that is all very well but she can not see to it, and pay the interest of the house, and rates and taxes, and I expect the rates and taxes will be in this month and Mother can not pay it so we shall have the brokers in, that will be the end of it, I expect. Miss Smith [probably a help hired to look after the children] and Mack are here now. I hope you do not think that when I write to you, I want to make mischief, but I do not quite see how we are going on like this for another five weeks, neither does Miss Smith and Dudley. Last night Dudley had to go round to Pullens [a local pub?] to fetch her out, and of course there was a row, and so he will not come tonight. Well I am afraid I must close now, love, I suppose Mother will write to you, so goodbye.

from your loving son Ronald.

Ronnie wrote again after they had moved house:

25, St. James Sq,
Holland Park West,
Dec. 22nd 1914.

Dear Dad,

I am afraid you will have to give up all hope of Mother leaving the drink alone. She has started again already, last night, she came in, in an awful state. Of course Smith has not been paid as Mother had no money in the morning and so had to keep the change of the half sovering [sic].

I really shall get the blues, if I stay there much longer, have come to no proper arrangement about Christmas day yet, so I do not know what is going to be done.

I will write again as soon as possible, cannot stop for more now.

Your loving son, Ronald. P.S. Dudley is writing.

Three days later Ronnie and his mother seem to be living apart.

25, St. James Sq
Holland Park West
Dec 25th 1914. Christmas Day.

Dear Dad,

Owing to a mistake about the address, we have sent on all letters to the Hippodrome, if there is one in Nottingham, so if they are not there, or if there is not a Hippodrome there, they will be, I expect, at the dead letter office. Miss Smith has written twice, and of course put the wrong address on the letters, and I have written and so has Dudley so I am sorry to have to say that when you get them, you will receive a bunch of bad news.

I hope that you will be able to come over on Sunday as it has been something terrible here, as I could not stand it any longer over there I came home leaving things as straight for Mother as I possibly could – now when we went over on Christmas day no dinner arranged or anything. Mother arranged with Miss Smith that she should get in all the necessary things in for today as she had had a cheque from Mr Alcock the other night, but nothing was there, Mother was in bed still, and still drunk. Whatever could have happened the night before, I do not know, the class [sic] cupboard was smashed, the class [sic] all over the floor, the dineroom [sic] was in simply a dreadful state – anybody would think there had been a cracksmens club there the night before. Well, anyway, to cut a very long story short, Dudley would not stay and went out with Mack, and of course Miss Smith followed, she could not do otherwise, under the circs, so I stayed as long as I could and straightened the house a bit and then I went, which was the only thing to be done, I had to persuade the booking clerk at the station to lend me two pence, as I was without money. Well I can not stay for more now, we are expecting the phone to ring any minute now. I hope you will spend a little better Christmas day than we.

Do try and come over, impossible to go on like this.

PS. Please excuse writing in great haste.

Your loving son, Ronald.

Dudley also wrote to their father:

You see, it's so difficult to explain all the 'little goings on' in a letter and it would only worry you if you knew everything, as you are unable to do much, but it's all very, very rotten, I can tell you. And I seem to feel the trouble now much more than I used too; and it all seems so <u>wickedly needless</u>.

To change the rotten subject. Miss Smith has bought me a very nice cake and the Enderlys have also <u>made</u> me one. So I'm alright for food!

I'm sending you on some Kolynos I bought today as I expect you've used the tube you took with you. I think I'd better stop now as I'm feeling shockingly tired and must get up in the morning early. Again thanking you really very much for your jolly decent letter and good wishes and sending same from myself.

Ever your son – Dudley.

Hope the play's running well and yourself.

P.S. I am glad you've written to Saville's partner as the money Mother was being allowed was of no use, and was being wickedly wasted.

I still have £1 – 4s. left of the money you sent, so there's that in an emergency.

Don't worry too much! if poss.

By 1917, my father, Ronnie, was working in the City as an insurance runner, earning seven shillings and sixpence a week. Then he saw an advert for a small part in a play at the Islington Empire. The part was that of an old man, but it paid three pounds a week. Thus he became an actor. His brother Dudley, meanwhile, had joined the army and been sent to France as a 2nd Lieutenant in the 5th Battalion, London Rifle Brigade. In a letter dated Sunday 12 August 1917, he wrote home:

My dear, dear '54 year old' Dad,

Hundreds of thanks for your topping, your 'perfectly-priceless-old' of 27th July – which I had 4 days ago. I loved reading it and hearing all the little, and big, things you'd been doing and the 'home' news, etc., etc., and I have re-read it many times since. — I've been longing and longing to hear from you for ages 'old Darling' and have longed, equally hard, to be allowed the time to write you and dear Mother, Ron and everyone else.

Before I go any further I must ask you to do one thing for me — as I shall not be able to write any-one else before Tuesday. Will you please, let dear Mother, Ron and Mack, Mrs P and the dear Enderlys all hear the little bits of 'news' I send you in this 'long-real-letter.'? — Don't forget — please. — I'll write of everything I can think of that I've done lately of interest to you all — and I'll only write of things that you may read absolutely word for word to them all from my letter! — Eh! — Tho' 'little details' of happy times in funny little parts of France where the war isn't — we'll discuss later over that cigar and limejuice! we're having in a few weeks together!! Jove! But I'm longing to talk to you again old darling!
NEWS.

First I must tell you of my latest achievement — We have been 'out at rest' since I came off my course at Warley. Various 'brigade sports' have been got up in order to make us believe the war is a good thing — SO IT IS!! Ha! Ha! (One must be cheerful!) — My platoon was entered for the close order drill, arms drill, best turn out, and guard mounting competition.

I had just 6 days to train 'em in. They hadn't been drilled or 'smartened up' since I left them for my course and was away 3 weeks altogether as you know. Also — on my return — I was made Batt: Musketry Officer, and this, as you'll guess, did not help me with 'time to spare' for the coaching of my men. However — this morning was the day! At 9.15 am I had 'em paraded in their 'joy rags'. — Managed to get them all new trousers, new puttees, and brilliantly fitting jackets! — (If you had any experience of Quartermasters and Regimental Taylors you'd agree this was 'some achievement' — 'Blood from a stone' — not in the same street!!) All their 'tin helmets' (and my own! which you'll agree suits me awf'ly well when I come home in it!) were re-covered with the real old 'sand-bag'. — Well — at 9.45am we 'moved off' to the

Competition ground – about 2 miles away and just muddy enough to ruin the polish on our boots, Cheer-oh! – On arrival here enter my C.O. (Colonel!) – Scene:- Typical French country (viz – grass and mud.) – Brigadiers, Staff Captains and other shining lights to the fore! My C.O. – ' 'orning Ward. Feel confident?' – Little tin-hatted Ward (with one pip!) 'Morning Sir, Oh! yes, sir, feeling A1, sir, and holding the field from the start, sir!'

My C.O. <u>'Good</u> ! (All C.O's say this!) Now, Ward, just take things calmly, don't hurry, <u>accuracy</u> – great thing accuracy – and mind they hold their heads up!'

L.T. Ward – 'Right, sir, Shall I move off? We're no. 2 in the list for show sir!' – and so on. Well – we 'moved off' and waited for just 10 mins or so before any chaps were called for. – Imagine me, standing between my C.O, Staff Capt and the Brig: with my poor old platoon lined up in front of us waiting for that well known shout from me of <u>'Shun'</u>. Anyhow, we started. – On the 'general turn out' we <u>beat every one</u> by scoring 25 (out of 30) against the second best platoon which got 19. Next, on the arms drill we scored <u>heavily</u> by a really 'posh' fix and unfix bayonets. – Like clock work – bless them! – Thirdly, in the close order drill, we marched off triumphantly after the general had said to me – 'A remarkably . . . an <u>extraordinarily</u> well drilled platoon, <u>my boy.'</u> Generals always call you 'my boy'!!) –

After that, of course I felt pretty bucked and told the men just how 'bucked' with them I was. We then did the guard-mounting stunt (this gave my poor old throat a bit of a rest as the corporals have to give the orders.) The result was announced – '2/5th London's platoon, officer 2nd Lieut Ward, winners: 94 points out of 100!' I was fearfully bucked, y'know, because it's a good thing to 'win' anything in front of a 'Brig': When I got the boys home I made a little 'talk' up and told 'em 'as I wasn't supposed to <u>kiss</u> 'em! I'd stand guarantee for as much 'posh' French beer tonight as they could manage before 'lights out'. Am getting the C.O. to give them tomorrow morning off – <u>in case</u> anyone oversleeps himself! Well, I knew you'd like to hear of all this and I've made it out 'full length' just so that you'll see – even out at rest – we <u>don't</u> waste our time!

Now, the next little news item is – about that L.E.A.V.E. – when I <u>do</u> get back, I don't think I shall have much difficulty in finding <u>you</u> and monopolizing you for 9 days and nights. – You didn't <u>really</u> think that after 6 or 7 months of this sort of fun I should come back to England and not be able to 'shake' with the 'old man'. – <u>If</u> you did – well you don't quite know 'old Duds' or what it's like to live from one day to another and not know whether you'll ever 'get that "Blighty" one' in time!

NO, Dad, <u>you'll</u> be there, sir, please! and so will <u>everyone</u> else I've been waiting to 'shake' with or kiss; (If I know how – Eh!). Leave has now opened with a rush again – four officers are going within the next 9 days – and this will about leave the path clear for myself and chums who came out with me, to go in about anytime from <u>a week hence to the end of September.</u>

I don't think any of you really realize, quite, that it is rather a 'novelty' to be out here six months without getting 'smacked', or 'stopping one of those big 'uns.' Now, do you!

Still, you shall hear everything you want to when I arrive at Waterloo. – Meanwhile, cheer-oh, always and remember it's a 'bang' war <u>really</u>! – All the Tommies out here say so, any way, and so I'm sure it's up to the 'dear ones' to <u>pretend</u> they like it too, y'know!

Give dearest Mother my greatest love and a million loving kisses for her and dear little(!) Babs! Jove! I'll go mad on her when I see her. Eh! <u>SO</u> let's hear from you <u>all</u> soon. now. – Meantime. <u>Cheer oh!</u> take care of yourself and tell the others to do so to [*sic*]. <u>More love to everyone</u>

Ever your devoted son <u>Duds.</u>

The next month a telegram arrived:

Post Office Telegrams:– OHMS: London.
Handed in at 5.02 pm Received here at 6.pm
To Ward 20a Clifton Villas
Warwick Avenue
T2488 MOST DEEPLY REGRET TO INFORM YOU THAT SECOND

LIEUTENANT D.T. WARD 5TH LONDONS WAS KILLED IN ACTION
SEPTEMBER 20TH.

2nd Lieutenant Dudley Ward, 5th
Battalion, London Rifle Brigade.

In the years after the war, my father and my grandfather were both on the
stage, though in rather different kinds of production. In 1921, for example, my
grandfather was billed at the Shepherd's Bush Empire as the performer of
'MASTERPIECES – the most delightful Musical Act in Vaudeville.'

But he still kept up appearances and on a beautiful sunny morning in
1923, attired in his usual immaculate morning dress, he walked into his
son's dressing room at the Savoy Theatre in the Strand, where Ronnie was
playing in Noël Coward's new play, *The Young Idea*, to ask him for a loan.
Ronnie obliged him with a few pounds, explaining that his creditors were
being very difficult. 'Ah,' said Theo, 'I must tell you what I've found to be
the most satisfactory solution for all concerned. I asked my milkman, my
grocer and my tailor and . . . oh, yes – and a chap from Steinway, to my
lodgings. Over tea, I said how very kind it was of them to come and then
explained that if they would be so kind as to accept how tricky things were

at present, they would soon get their money, if they would be patient enough to agree to accept a small amount each month. They all seemed quite happy with my suggestion and we parted the best of friends.' Theo laughed. 'Sadly they never got their money – my position was too precarious!' Soon after he went to see his tailor to thank him for his forbearance. His tailor said, 'Ah, Mr Ward, perhaps you would care to step this way' and he was measured for another suit.

My father was fond of such stories (others involved mix-ups over chorus girls, tipping one's hat at the wrong one, etc.), but they concealed a sad decline. Towards the end of his life, Theo played a few wrong notes during a bottom-of-the-bill appearance at the Holborn Empire. There were shouts of 'drunkard' and he was booed off the stage. In fact, he'd had stroke. He recovered and lived in a room in Camden Town. Ronnie paid his bills; when his daughter, Beryl, went to see him he was mostly near to tears.

In May 1935 Theo died of a cerebral haemorrhage. Men from the Steinway company came to collect their piano, for which no payments had ever been

Theo.

Twice nightly.

17

received. I was six. I can remember meeting him only once. As for his wife, my grandmother, I was never allowed to meet her. Until I was twenty I assumed she was dead, or perhaps somewhere far away, like Australia. Instead she was living with her daughter, Beryl (whom I had also never met), in rooms not far from the cinema in Kentish Town, where Beryl worked as an usherette. There, in 1949, she died – I came to know the details later. One morning Beryl leaned across the bed they shared, touched her mother and found her rather cold. Beryl was a simple woman, 'not quite right' as they said in those days, and she couldn't understand why her mother wouldn't wake up. Thinking that she was ill or just tired, Beryl dressed herself and went for a walk. Lunchtime came and mother was still asleep. It was a matinée day at the cinema, so she went off to do her usheretting. 'Mother will be better when I get back,' she said to herself. When she got back in the evening, her mother was still sleeping, and still cold. She tried to wake her. She sat by the bed and cried and then got in the bed and cried. She tried to sleep: 'I'll get a doctor in the morning.' But in a little while she became very frightened. She jumped out of bed and rushed outside. She couldn't see anyone about. She went to a bus stop and when a bus came along she waved at it and got on and stammered to the conductor, 'My mummy's ill. I don't know what to do.' The conductor stopped the bus and took her to a doctor. The doctor came back with her. The doctor told her that her mother had died.

I've always felt sad that I was never allowed to meet Grandmother Marie, but by the time my father was nine her alcoholism had become an irreversible condition, from which she only recovered when she died that morning. As for Beryl, she eventually recovered from her ordeal and made a new life for herself in Brighton. She loved to go dancing at the local club, where she met two husbands, and outlived them both. When she died, aged seventy-seven in her council flat on 12 December 1989, she was in the throes of yet another serious relationship. She gained her happiness through her simplicity.

So much for the Wards, of whom, my father apart, I saw and knew so little. My grandparents on my mother's side – the Willoughbys – were much better

The Six Willoughbys of Shouldham Street: from left, Phil, Jessica, Harold, Ena, Clarence and Grace.

known to me. My grandfather Harold Willoughby was born one of six children at 12 Shouldham Street, Marylebone, where his parents made straw bonnets. There were three boys and three girls and all the boys became musicians – Phil on the violin, Clarence on the cello and grandfather Harold on the viola.

Harold was born in 1881 and had a lively late Victorian childhood, which he was fond of remembering. By the time he was twelve, he'd become a valued member of a local gang that roamed the streets of Marylebone playing their favourite game: knocking off the stove-pipe hats of passing gentlemen with balls of horse shit, which they made with great care from the piles of horse dung left on the streets of a still-horse-drawn city. Music made him respectable. He married Ethel Walker, one of the many daughters of Dr Augustus Walker (BA, Mus. Doc.), and the couple set up home in a rented three-storey Victorian semi-detached house at the bottom of a wide curved hill that was Ritherdon Road, Tooting, south London. Chatsby was written in stained glass above the front door. The word has theatrical associations – actors in rehearsal would use it when they couldn't remember the right word or the right name, as non-theatricals might say 'thingamabob'. Whether my grandparents knew of this association I can't say, but the word has followed me throughout my life. I've named dogs after it, and more than one house, and I guess that to me it must imply happiness.

Chatsby in stained glass above the door of 37 Ritherdon Road.

Here they raised their children, my Uncle Robert and my mother, Peggy, who was born in 1907.

As a child I was often taken to this house. From the pavement, a wooden gate opened on to a small garden with a broad tiled pathway, the tiles of which were continued into the hall of the house. The back garden was a little bigger than the front, with old brick walls surrounding a small patch of grass with a gravel path running down one side. I have several early memories. It was outside the scullery window, behind which Granny was doing the washing up, that my sister survived me bashing her on the head with a cricket bat. Granny saw me do it. I was punished – there is a memory of tears. Inside the house, on a brass tray-table in the hall by the stairs, stood a small brass cobra. Once I picked the snake up and it fell out of my hands. It rang out like a bell as it hit the tiles. There was a telephone on a window sill at the bottom of the stairs. Once Grandfather Harold ran naked down the stairs to answer its ring. Holding the phone with one hand, he put the earpiece to his ear with the other and leaned against the sill. When the maid came down the stairs in front of him, he crossed one leg over the other and went on talking.

I suppose there was something of the bohemian in him. He was fond of telling the story of an incident that had happened when he was supervising – from his seat at the piano – the auditioning of musicians for jobs in the resident orchestra at the newly built Earls Court Exhibition Halls. Councillors of the London County Council were sitting in the front row. It was a habit on occasions like this that, for luck, a member of the orchestra would quietly whisper at the conclusion of a phrase the last line of a dirty song. The audition began and, as they played, it dawned on them that a whisperer had not been appointed. The phrase came up and, fearing nobody would say it, what should have been a whisper became a shout of 'Who's the bugger that fucked the cat?' Silence. Without a glance they packed up their instruments. Not a word was spoken until they reached the nearest pub.

My mother began her career as a dancer in her early teens, when she toured the country in a musical act with Harold, her father, at the piano. In 1923 she was dancing in cabaret at the Trocadero in London. Around this time she and my father met when they were auditioning for André Charlot, the great 'revue' producer of the period. She was sixteen and he was twenty-three, and they both won small parts in *Charlot's Revue of 1924*, which starred Noël Coward, Gertrude Lawrence, Beatrice Lillie and Jack Buchanan, and opened in New York at the Times Square Theatre. Jessie Matthews, later the darling of English musicals, was in the chorus with Peggy and for a time my father dithered between the two, until he decided he preferred Peggy's musical taste (or so he used to insist) and they fell in love.

Ronnie wrote from the Grand Union Hotel, 32nd Street, New York:

Dear Dad,
There is one thing I'm afraid that I am going to find out and that is that America is not at all artistically inclined. People apparently go to hear Kreisler or Paderewski, etc., because 'it's done'. All our subtle ideas

for instance in our revue are not understood and anything slow in the way of music, such as Noël Coward's 'Parisiene Pierrot' (you remember?), apparently there is not enough 'pep' in it for them. In other words everything has to be fast and furious. Their musical comedy orchestras have at least 5 or 6 saxophones in them!

Towards the end of 1924, Ronnie left the show and went to Australia with the Dion Boucicault company, and Peggy was writing letters to him beginning 'My Dearest Own Darling Thing' and ending them 'All my heart and soul – Pegs, Boo, Baby' with kisses at the bottom – 'Thousands of them which will penetrate to your lips from mine'. When the Charlot Revue closed, Peggy went into another Charlot show in London, but not for long. By early 1925, in spite of opposition from Charlot, she had booked her passage to Australia.

Charlot sent a cable to Ronnie:

PEGGY IS IN AWFUL QUANDARY – WILLING RELEASE HER – AM SURE SHE LOVES YOU DEARLY BUT SHE IS GETTING FIRST CHANCE WITH ME AND PROGRESSING WELL – STOP – BAD FOR HER PROFESSIONALLY TO LEAVE LONDON NOW – YOU ARE BOTH YOUNG – IF YOU WAIT ANOTHER YEAR FEEL SURE SHE WILL WAIT FOR YOU – BE SENSIBLE AND CABLE HER ACCORDINGLY – CHARLOT.

To which Ronnie cabled back:

REALISE BOTH YOUNG – STILL YOUNG IN 12 MONTHS – PEGGY EASILY CONTINUE WITH YOU THEN – URGENTLY NEED HER HERE – WARD.

So Peggy cabled Ronnie for fifty pounds and left for Melbourne, Australia. They were married on 20 April 1925. On 13 February 1927 my sister, Patricia Rosemary Irene, was born. Three days later, Ronnie wrote to his father:

The most awful tragedy to us is that we have to make the biggest sacrifice in our lives. Having gone thoroughly into matters, we find that, either Peggy and I part for, perhaps, two years, or we part with little babe. Well, as there doesn't appear to be a bean in either family we have decided that we must stop out here and make some money. So Peggy has signed on to stop for six months and six months option; by which time I shall know how I stand. As it is impossible (apart from expense) to travel an infant about the country, Mrs Willoughby [Peggy's mother] is taking it [sic] home at the early age of 5 weeks and the mite will be properly cared for and looked after by a trained nurse & superintended by the family and you, until we can come home. This is, of course an awful wrench for Peggy after all she's gone through, but she realized that it will be all for the best in the end. How we are going to part with our lovely little baby – I don't know.

MW *circa* six months, on my mother's knee, Tooting Bec Common.

Peggy didn't return to England until she was pregnant with me. I was conceived in Australia and born in a nursing home in Streatham, south London, on 15 January 1929. Ronnie followed a few months later and Peggy took her father, Harold, to Southampton docks to meet him for the first time. He was high above them, leaning over the rails of the liner and laughing and gesticulating insanely to them. 'Solid ivory from the neck up,' said Harold. The marriage was already faltering. In 1930 my father was in a play called *Let Us Be Gay* with Tallulah Bankhead at the Lyric Theatre. Fatal, of course. She and Ronnie had an affair – she was another person Ronnie didn't marry. Outside the stage door of the Lyric one night and not wishing to publicize their liaison, Ronnie hung back from the crowd surrounding Tallulah's car. Her voice rang out: 'Get in the fucking car, Ronnie.' I have two signed photographs of Tallulah in my possession: one by Dorothy Wilding signed to Ronnie and another by Cecil Beaton signed to Peggy. I've often wondered if Tallulah, who was known to jump both sides of the fence, didn't fancy my mother too.

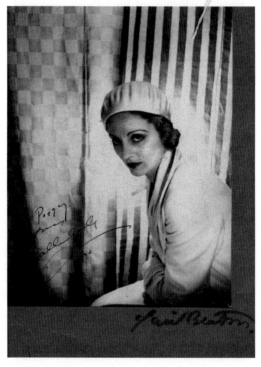

To Peggy from Tallulah.

3

I was three and my sister five when our parents separated and we were sent to boarding school, officially Gloucester House School, which comprised two Victorian houses at the corner of a crossroads in Ealing, west London. To us, it was always Miss Mann's, the name of the fierce old lady who ran it. She had black-rimmed glasses and a mass of white hair piled up on her head, held in place with large black hairpins. But she was gentle. I once nearly knocked her over when I ran to hug my father at the other end of the gym – he'd arrived to take Pat and me on an excursion – and I remember that she smiled at me kindly. The school was handily placed for the Ealing Studios, where Ronnie was sometimes filming, and he would turn up in his red-wheeled, two-seater MG to take us to tea. The only thing I remember about these outings is the desperate sadness I felt watching his car disappear round the corner.

In 1932 Peggy was singing and dancing in Noël Coward's *Words and Music* and Ronnie was with Gerald du Maurier in *Behold We Live* at the St James's Theatre. The next year he was with Marie Tempest in *The Old Folks at Home*. He now had a regular girlfriend, Betty Baskcomb, whose father was an old friend of his father (they met in Paris during Theo's time there in 1909) and who, when the thirty-year-old Ronnie took up with her in 1931, was all of sixteen. Betty would take us in her car for tea at the Maids of Honour, by Kew Gardens. She was very kind to us and continued to be so, in spite of Ronnie's refusal to marry her for many years (he eventually gave in, in 1948).

During the summer holidays, Gloucester House School decamped to Seasalter in Kent, which was then a little old village by the sea and is now buried under bungalows and caravans. There, in 1936, my grandfather and granny came to see us.

Seasalter seemed to us a wonderful place. My sister and I would race over the sands to the distant sea, running and splashing in the pools the tide had left behind. It was also on this holiday that I was first excited by sex – the incident is etched in my memory. Everybody had gone down with measles except me, so I was quarantined to sleep in the garage with one of the mistresses, a Miss Freeman. When she came to bed she started to undress, but noticing that I was awake and idly watching her she told me to hide under my bedclothes at once. I did, and through the holes of my eiderdown saw her taking off her skirt and a pair of tight-fitting directoire knickers in pale green silk, which sort of hissed as she drew them down her legs. I have rarely had sex out of my mind for more than a few minutes in the seventy years since.

Seasalter, 1936, Pat (my sister), third row back first from left, MW front row third from left, Miss Mann, fourth row back third from right.

In September 1936 a new play and a new mistress for Ronnie: the play was *George and Margaret* by Gerald Savory, the mistress was Jane Baxter, the leading lady. A glorious woman with a soft, deep voice. Ronnie was very much in love. She started a savings account for Pat and me with ten shillings each and took me out for a treat in her black Ford V8 convertible. We pulled up at the lights at Tower Bridge. I was riveted to my seat as I watched the road in front slowly rise and form a block of tarmac in front of me. Bits of paper and things that people threw away

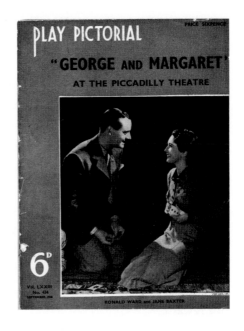

started slipping down the gutters. I was fascinated by a packet of Players' cigarettes gathering speed as it slid down the left-hand gutter to join a pile of rubbish at the bottom. I remembered that when, some time in the 1970s, forty and more years later, I photographed Jane Baxter when she was rehearsing a play at Colchester. After the photographs we stood on the stage chatting for a short while. She was still as lovely, but the magic I remembered feeling, waiting for Tower Bridge to close, had gone. Pat and I had so wanted our father to marry her. He didn't. Now she was married to an army officer.

In 1937 Pat and I went to school in Richmond. I was eight and she was ten. Pat's school, called the Old Vicarage, was halfway up Richmond Hill and looked like a castle. It had a huge front door, opening on to a great hall with carpets and large black and white tiles, on which a great floppy Great Dane lay. The school was run by Miss Jesse Cross, who was very kind to me when I was allowed to visit my sister. Pat loved her school and I hated mine. Her school was warm and friendly and echoed with convivial voices – voices that asked you about yourself. My school was rowdy and hostile, though it was housed in a very beautiful, double-fronted Georgian house, with a wonderful mature wisteria winding round its white windows. There were some day boys and some boarders. I, of course, was a boarder. The school had two headmasters – a Mr Butler and a Mr Wigan.

Mr Wigan was a kindly man with ginger hair and gold-rimmed spectacles who once took me to Twickenham in his new two-seater Riley. If he had to beat you, he used a soft slipper on your shorts. Mr Butler, on the other hand, was not at all kindly. Everything about him suggested severity: his horn-rimmed glasses, his black shoes, his black pinstripe suit, his black pipe filled with Tom Long tobacco. If, during breakfast, he noticed you with your elbows on the table, he would catch your eye and crook his forefinger. Then he would stroke the crooked forefinger with his other forefinger. This meant that you were to be beaten. He enjoyed beating the boys, usually on a Saturday morning, when the week's list of vices and virtues were added up under a system of 'stars and stripes'. If a boy had three stripes against his name he was awarded a beating. Three stars meant no beating, which was assumed to be the equivalent of a reward.

Mr Butler beat his boys in his study, a large room on the second floor. You waited your turn in the corridor, watching sobbing boys leaving the room and clutching their trousers. His desk, on which lay the cane, was by the window. There was a chair in front of the desk. He told you to take your trousers down and bend over the back of the chair. You grasped the rails under the seat and, even now, I can still feel the searing pain as the cane hit my bare bottom. Once, I tried to prepare myself for the blows by clenching my buttocks but Mr Butler ordered me to relax and waited for me to do so before continuing with the beating. In the summer, when the windows were left open, you could hear the swish of the cane as you crossed the forecourt of the school, and you thought, 'Hell, I'm glad that's not me.'

There were outings. One day we walked down Richmond Hill, in line through the town and then on to the green and up a wide flight of steps, through a foyer and into quiet blackness. A square of light slowly spread among the hundreds of seats. I was in the auditorium of the Richmond Theatre. We were told to go up on the stage. I felt my way up dimly lit steps. The deep quiet persisted. From the stage, the seats receded into the gloom at the back of the stalls. The smell of size, the stuff that tautens the scenery flats, was heavy. It was all very exciting. I was going to play one of the ten little boys in Agatha Christie's play called *Ten Little Niggers*. It has since been retitled twice — first as *Ten Little Indians* and second as *And Then There Was None*. There was only one performance, and I remember nothing of it.

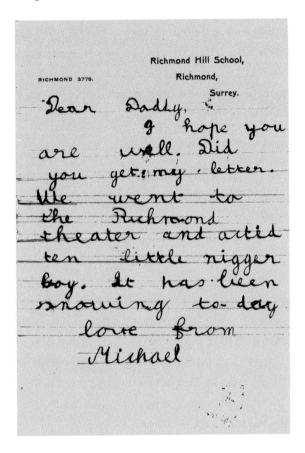

Richmond Hill School,
Richmond,
Surrey.

RICHMOND 3779.

Dear Daddy,
    I hope you are well. Did you get my letter. We went to the Richmond theater and acted ten little nigger boy. It has been snowing to-day love from Michael

Sometimes we went further afield. One sunny afternoon, as the school crocodiled its way through Hyde Park to the Science Museum, I spotted BXF 644, the number plate of my father's black Humber Vogue car. It was parked by the Serpentine, just before the bridge. My heart leapt and I looked all around to see if I could see him. I asked the master if I could wait in case my father came back to the car. He said no and asked me if I knew when he might be returning to the car. I couldn't answer. All I knew was that the car gave me a glimpse of warmth, freedom and happiness: things that holidays would bring, if holidays were spent outside the school, which was by no means guaranteed. As the end of each term got nearer I would try to read portents in events. If certain incidents happened in a particular order it could mean that either Ronnie or Peggy would come to the school to collect me for the holidays. A different order of events could mean that I would be staying at the school. It was my way of praying.

My heart couldn't cope if I had to stay at school. I just broke down. And then, after a while, I adjusted to the circumstances and enjoyed whatever the holiday had to offer. Life was an emotional circle that didn't really stop circling till I was into my forties (and even now there's a ripple or two). I was a rather stupid, happy boy, who on the surface was able to adjust to whatever happened to him.

For the spring holidays in 1937 Pat and I went to Brighton. Over the road from the boarding house which Granny Willoughby had taken for our holidays was a bus garage. I wandered idly round, savouring the smell of petrol, enchanted by the rhythmic beat of the engines. I was already in love with cars and almost anything else that moved on a road. It was a wonderful holiday. Mummy came down for a few days and Grandfather came down for a weekend. Ronnie was touring in *George and Margaret*, and we met him, Jane Baxter and Daphne Rye, one of H. M. Tennant's casting directors, on the beach near the pier. Daphne always wore red-framed dark glasses, so I never really knew what she looked like. (Later, in 1953, when she still worked for H. M. Tennant, and I was understudying David Tomlinson in *The Little Hut* at the Lyric Theatre, I embarrassed myself and her by saying, apropos of nothing, that Edith Evans was my god-mother – she affected total lack of interest.)

Ronnie and I were drying ourselves inside a bathing hut – he said, 'Extraordinary thing– I've just dried myself and I'm still wet – all very peculiar.' The way he said it was so funny, I fell about the hut laughing.

Granny took us on the beach at Rottingdean. On a circular staircase leading up from the beach we passed some dirty-looking children. I said to Granny, 'I always hold my breath when I pass people like that.' She slapped my face and told me how they were just as good as us, if not better. 'But Granny,' I said, 'they smell.' Another slap, then silence till we got back to the boarding house.

254, Eastern Road, Brighton, April 1937.

Dear Dad,

   I hope you are well. I am so sorry you did not come Sunday. I have
drawn Micky Mouse in Patricia's autograph book and have written – 'to
Pat the Big Sausage – MANY HAPPY RETURNS OLD BEAN LOVE
FROM MICHAEL

Christmas 1937, a letter from my sister to Ronnie:

Darling Daddy,

   Have you had the christmas card yet, that I sent you, I have had a
lovely Xmas this year darling.

   Why I really wrote was because in Michael's letter he forgot to put
that he wants some new outdoor shoes, because he cannot posobly
wear them again there is a nail in them and they are worn out, and
yesterday we went to the pictures and he limped all the way in them.

   I must stop now darling because michael is getting on my nerves,
he's awful.

   Good By darling, Love Pat.XXXXXXXXXXX.

In 1938, Ronnie was filming in *St. Martin's Lane*.

A still from *St. Martin's Lane*: Ronnie, Rex Harrison and Vivien Leigh.

In 1939 Betty Baskomb, who had been enticing Ronnie to marry her for the previous eight years, took me out from Richmond Hill School to her home in Finchley for tea. We were in the garden and I borrowed her Box Brownie camera to take pictures of her. She said she would enter the photos into a competition in the *Daily Mail*. No further word was heard.

In March 1939 I left Richmond Hill School for the Easter holidays and never returned. Great-Aunt Louisa took me in at her 'Board Residence' establishment in Myddelton Square, near the Angel, Islington, which was run by her daughters, Jan and Ivy. It was a five-storey terraced house tucked into the corner of a lovely Georgian square which had enormously wide roads made of wooden blocks covered in tar. I roller-skated hanging on to the spare wheel of taxis as they slowed to go round the square, until I was either discovered by the cabbie or his cab's speed compelled me to let go.

My sex life consisted of stealthily climbing the dark lino-covered stairs to see if I could catch a glimpse of Jan and Ivy taking their weekly bath together. As I peered through a small window at the top of the bathroom door, they would call out, 'Don't be so silly, Michael.'

In the basement, a corridor led to a small room which had a copper basin with a space for a fire underneath it, for washing clothes. At the other side of

Betty Baskcomb by MW.   MW taking Betty Baskcomb.

the basement, the front room looked out on to a small paved yard with black railings at street level. A rickety door led to the coal hole under the pavement. The circular cast-iron cover in the pavement above was removed with a clank and the coal was poured out of black bags stiffened by coal dust. The coalman's voice, cried, 'Cooaaal, Cooaaaal — *Buy a bag,*' as the clip-clop of the horse's hoofs faded down the street.

In the hall, a black, separate earpiece telephone stood on an old butler's tray. The number was Terminus 1911, and those numbers might have stood for the era that still possessed the house. There were gas lamps in all the rooms. Some of them had two delicate chains which see-sawed a bar of intricately patterned brass, which when pulled turned the gas on or off. The glowing pilot light lit the gas and made the mantle incandescent, giving out a yellowy-white light, shining through a pink china shade. It burned with a quiet roar.

Great-Aunt Louisa, my Grandfather Theo's sister, lived in a room on the ground floor which looked out on to the square. She was a sweet and gentle old lady whose eyes, when open, were nearly closed. We had an enchanting relationship — we both thought the other very funny. Sometimes I'd knock on the door of her room when she had still to finish dressing, but she would say,

'Come in, Michael,' and sit with me in her black satin slip, her uncoiled silvery hair reaching down to the back of her knees. We talked, laughed and enjoyed each other's company. Looking at us over her gold-rimmed pince-nez, Louisa would chuckle and call my sister Pat and me 'the Bisto Kids' because we could impersonate the Bisto advert, sticking our chins out, smelling imaginary wisps of gravy and hhhmming at the same time.

Round the corner in Chadwell Street, I took piano lessons in rooms above a newsagent's (soon to be obliterated by a bomb). I tried to practise, but I was too lazy. At night I lay in bed at the top of the house and read the adverts on the front page of *The Times* until it grew dark – understanding very little beyond three-letter words. The strange noises of London frightened me, even the cries of the newsvendors, '*Star, News* and *Standard*', which drifted from the Angel.

What was to be done with me? On 30 April my father wrote to my mother: 'I haven't the remotest idea what I am going to do with Michael – still all that and worse has to be faced when I return.' Then one night Ivy took me to Euston station. Ivy was the least pretty but by far the most practical of Louisa's daughters, with a very forceful personality, who continually pronounced on the problems that beset our family as well as the world in general. She chained-smoked De Reske Minor cigarettes and between puffs often quoted Shakespeare: I gathered she was a disappointed actress and had had a thwarted love affair. That night, however, it was Euston that interested me more than Ivy. The huge glass-and-steel-girdered roof was full of smoke, the platforms full of people. Whistles blew, doors slammed, steam hissed out of large black and shiny locomotives, which had names above their wheels on a curved plaque, brass letters on a red background. Ivy hustled and dragged me along the platform and put me into a carriage. The door slammed and she kissed me several times through the window. I sat back in the compartment – alone, bewildered, excited. It was after eleven at night. My instruction from Ivy was to get out at Leighton Buzzard station, an hour or so up the line, where I'd be met. And sure enough, there on the platform was a tall man who greeted me by name and then drove me in a Morris saloon to a large house in the country. I woke up the next morning and looked out of the window and saw the yard of Ashby Farm. I had been evacuated, though the war was still several months away.

*

Mr and Mrs Ashby owned the farm, but it was their son, Walter, who'd met me at the station, and their daughter, Muriel, a good-looking girl in her early twenties, who was given the job of looking after me. Thereafter, I woke up to the noise of cart horses stamping on the brick floor of the stable block. I was up at five in the mornings helping to harness them and back them into the shafts of their carts. Two of them became my special friends. I rode or rather slid all over the back of Captain, a big shire horse with a long main and tail, and his friend Bob, who was smaller and with a bobbed tail. There was a brand-new tractor, but nobody used it.

I lay alone on the straw in a great oak barn, watching the chickens and an enormous fat sow suckling her ten babies. I wandered across fields and sat on a fence, keeping still until a herd of cows slowly came up to sniff me. Across the fields in another farmhouse I discovered a beautiful girl called Anne with whom I fell in love. She was blonde with broad cheekbones and a loving smile. I remember from my first visit the dilapidation of her parents' farmhouse, and the roughly hewn stones of the dark corridor that led to the kitchen. A sheep dog barked and growled at me from the corner.

Anne became the first girl I really missed.

I wrote to my mother:

> Dear Mummy, Thank you for your letter, I expect you were startled
> when I came down here of a sudden, lets hope war doesn't come. I was
> riding the horses all day yesterday and I helped shift the cowe one field
> to another. There is not much to say because I have only been away a
> couple of days. Love Mike.

September the third was a bright, brittle morning. At eleven the Ashby family gathered in the living room and I was told to be quiet as the prime minister was about to speak. The wireless was tuned in and Chamberlain said, '. . . we are therefore at war with Germany.' I had never known grown-ups so quiet. A few minutes later the silence was broken by a strange wailing sound a long way off. It was the air-raid warning. Instead of taking shelter, everybody rushed outside to look up at the sky. We saw nothing. The all-clear sounded as we searched for German planes.

From Ashby Farm, 11 September 1939:

Dear Mummy,

I hope you are well. I had a letter from Aunty Betty (Betty Baskcomb) at the time I got yours. Please tell Daddy to send me a letter. Have you heard Aunty Betty has joined the Auxiliry Fire Service and is driving the chief of them. A few days ago I went for a picnic at the top of the Beacon. I have rides on the horses. I hope we win the war. Give my love to the rest of them. – Love Mike.

During this first quiet period of the war (when my father rather surprisingly joined the Home Guard) I went back to Myddelton Square for a short while and then I was taken to a new school in Bexhill-on-Sea in Sussex. My father drove down with the actor John Le Mesurier and Mesurier's girlfriend, June Melville (whose father owned the Princes Theatre, now known as the Shaftesbury), and we had tea at the town's De La Warr Pavilion, which seemed like a liner and impressively new, after which I was taken to Lake House School near Cooden Beach. The lump in my throat got bigger and bigger. I stood with the headmaster on the doorstep saying goodbye. As my father's car went down the drive, I broke loose from the headmaster's grip and, sobbing and crying, ran after the car and jumped on the back of it.

At the end of the Christmas term, I wrote to my mother:

Dear Mum,

I hope you are well. I am returning to London on Tuesday, if I stay at Myddelton for a few days with nothing to do, please could I come and see me. Thank you very much for the five shillings. Love Mike
XXXXXXXXXXXXX

And again to her in May 1940:

Dear Mum,

This afternoon we saw twelve Westland Lysanders, a model of which I have got. I am taking shooting here so if a German parachutist lands in Bexhill I can [take a] pot at him . . . Love Mike.

And the next month:

Dear Mum,

I hope you are well. Thank you for this lovely writing pad, I have made a crude frame for the picture of you, one of the boys thought Ginger Rogers was a man. We fly the Union Jack evry day now as there is a war on, it looks gay. Just outside the gate was a big gun a heavy howitzer. Love Mike.

My mother, Peggy Willoughby, in *New Faces* at the Comedy Theatre, London, 1940, and another dancer – Ginger Rogers.

They Dance

Ginger Rogers, the dancing screen star, with her Afghan. One of her latest films is " The Primrose Path."

Peggy Willoughby dances in " New Faces " at the Comedy Theatre.

In the summer of 1940 I stayed at my sister's school. It had been evacuated to a beautiful Georgian house, Prestwood Lodge, standing in spacious grounds near Great Missenden, Buckinghamshire. It had a large white, detached conservatory. I spent the summer holidays there and I had a room at the top of the house, from which I looked at the moon on windy, cloudy nights and watched it dance through the branches of the fir tree outside my window. In the room next door to me were three girls, Tish, Zena and my sister Pat.

Although it was the holidays, a lot of the girls didn't go home because of the war. They seemed to be much more conscious of me being a boy than I was of them being girls. Perhaps there were too many of them for me. We had marvellous bike rides and games in the grounds and outbuildings. The evenings were often spent listening to and performing music. One evening I was chosen to sing the male part in a musical play the girls were putting on. I have never been able to sing since without acute embarrassment. When my part came only a high-pitched tinkly sound came out as my voice hadn't broken yet. All the girls laughed at me. My face burned and I ran out of the room.

When the air-raid siren sounded we gathered up our bedclothes, went down the stone steps to the basement and huddled together on the floor. I was next to a girl called June and as I lay by her I desperately wanted to touch her. I could feel the heat of her and the tickle of the blankets when she moved. My hand moved very, very slowly towards her. It must have been several minutes before I was near to actually touching her and I thought, I'll just put my hand on her and then keep quite still. She moved and I pretended that I had touched her accidentally. I don't remember kissing anyone during my stay at the school. Perhaps just a fleeting brush on a cheek.

From Prestwood Lodge, Great Missenden, summer 1940:

> Dear Mum —
>   Last night it rained bombs the nasty Nazis came over and big bomb fell near and shook Pat out of bed but I slept through it all. Love Mike.

Harold and Granny's house, 37 Ritherdon Road, had been bombed.

Dear Mum,

I hope you are well.

3 bombs fell in Missenden and I have been inside the craters of two of them, they all just missed the railway line. Poor old Ritherdon Road.

Nearly all the windows in the High Street, in Great Missenden were broken two of the bombs which exploded directly they hit the ground the other was a time bomb which exploded 2 hours afterwards.

The other night we saw a plane caught in a searchlight but it was british.

Can't think of anything else. Love Mike.

Letter from Pat to our mother, December 1940:

Darling Mummy,

How are you and everybody? Daddy came down last Sunday and Mike went on Tuesday. Did you see him before he went to Wales? I was very sorry when he went, and so was he in a way. We hardly quarelled at all, all the hols. I suppose we are growing up. All my love to all. Love Pat

Suddenly I was living in another world. I'd been evacuated again, this time to North Wales. I hadn't seen mountains before and there they were, staggeringly large against the pink sky, framed in the train window. Lapping at their feet were great long stretches of water. The lakes or lyns of Wales. I was so excited – it was all so wondrous. My school had been billeted to a hotel, the Royal Victoria Hotel, Llanberis. Such luxury – vast areas of blue carpet, staircases as wide as roads, double doors everywhere. Comfortable chairs and tables for us to work on by windows looking out on to stretches of lawn surrounded by trees.

In our first break from lessons I ran out across a wide pebbled path, down a steep bank of short grass, then into the trees to a stream with fish swimming in deep pools of clear water. I knelt down on my bare knees, on the squashy, wet moss, and swished the cold water. I was, at that moment, enraptured with the world as never before.

There was some talk of our being sent far away from the war to Canada. Letter to Peggy, July 1940:

The Royal Victoria Hotel, Llanberis, N. Wales.

Dear Mum,

Excuse pencil – not allowed ink in hotel. I hope you are well. Sorry I have not written before.

I suppose you know we have evacuated up here to the above address don't you. Well it is awfully nice up here we can play bowls, fishing, golf, tennis and go climbing mountains. Yesterday we went half way up Mt Snowdon but you needn't worry about me falling over the edge because Mr Williams takes FULL precautions.

I have not been very well because of the air but I am alright now.

There [are] gards garding the road and they stop everybody that passes including lorries and cars. Please could you write soon. Thank you very much for the PO you sent me.

We have about 170 soldiers staying at the Hotel. They have just arrived from Dunkirk, we watch one of them drilling nearly every morning 1 of them we have made friends with and also a few others, he let me look at his gun and I loaded and reloaded it, it had nothing in it except air so it was alright, they are drilling now. I do not like the idea of going to Canada at all, but if I have to go I have to go and that's that. Worse luck.

Love Mike. XXXXXXXX

And from Pat to Peggy:

It was a shock when I read about Canada. I'm now going to ask you a long string of questions.

If we go to Canada, will we go before the summer holidays are over roughly? (I don't expect you know any of the answers yourself, but still, I must ask somebody, I feel so curious) Is Michael coming here for the hols at the end of the term, or are we both going somewhere else? Do you know the name of place where we are going?

I wish you would come down so that we could talk over things, I feel quite lost. I don't even know whether I want go or not, not that that matters because (it) is for you and Daddy to decide. I hate the feeling of leaving you and everybody in England to be bombed and Mike and I safe miles away in Canada, and I hate the thought of leaving this school, and starting again, even if I am coming back again afterwards, I hope. Oh! I wish you were here to talk to, I can't write everything on paper.

Have you heard from Mike? Do you know whether he is happy? I do hope so. I expect he is. He hasn't written to me for years, all this term in fact. Please will you send his address? Thank you darling.

Goodbye and <u>do please</u> come soon soon darling. (Love to all)

All my love – Pat – XXXXXXXXXXXXX (XXXXXXXXX – for Daddy)

A little after Pat writing this letter a ship carrying evacuee children, the *SS City of Benares*, was torpedoed and sunk in mid-Atlantic.

The Germans tried several times to bomb Llanberis. We soon discovered why: we were sitting next to one of the largest ammunition dumps in the country! People said they were after the big slate quarry by Llyn Padarn, but it wasn't slate they were after, it was the explosives under the lake. We had to move six or seven miles over the pass of Llanberis to the Pen-y-Gwryd Hotel, which stands at the junction of two roads high up in the mountains, alone except for one house where the hotel owner lived. There was a small lake the other side of the road on which we boated and skated. We were cut off for three weeks by ten-foot-deep snow drifts one winter. It was quite extraordinary to be so alone among all those mountains, in the velvet silence, in between the storms. And in the summer I loved jumping from one huge rock to another where great boulders and slabs of slate had come to rest on the mountainside behind the school after some earthquake many years ago.

We slept three beds to a small room, jammed together, and we were woken by the headmaster at about seven to go swimming in the small lake at the back of the hotel, sometimes breaking the thin ice.

In spite of the rain and wind, we had a wonderful time in Snowdonia. The headmaster organized us into three troops of Boy Scouts. We did all the things expected of Boy Scouts, like tying knots and pretend-fighting with our long Scout staffs. We built three large stone huts by a river (which are still used by farmers to shelter their sheep) and a football pitch beside the lake – the last took us a long time, and I found the work very tiring, and miserable, because I didn't like football. When it was finished we used it for gym classes and matron embarrassed me by telling me that, when I jumped up and down, my breasts wobbled like a girl's. During Latin class one day in March 1941, I was dreaming away, gazing out of the window, watching the rain squalls being blown along the mountainside, when a shout went up: 'Look, it's a Jerry.' The class leapt to the window and we saw the fuselage of a German twin-engined bomber, a Heinkel-111, being towed away on a low-loader lorry. It had been shot down, presumably while bombing the ammunition dump in Llanberis. We jumped to the window, cheering and shouting anti-German insults. The master brought his fists on to the table with a crash and shouted, 'SILENCE.' We quietly sat in our places. He said, 'That was the most disgusting display of stupidity I've seen for a long time.' There was silence. He went on, 'There were men in that aircraft who were most likely killed or badly wounded. They may have wives and children at home, just like your mothers and sisters and brothers. How would you like it if you heard that your father had been killed while flying over Germany? They were attacking us and we had to defend ourselves and we were lucky enough to have shot them down, hopefully before they were able to kill or wound any of us. You must never gloat and cheer over your enemies' defeat – just be thankful it wasn't the other way round.'

I was so happy and astonished one day in the summer of 1941 to see my father in the road outside the window. He'd come to see me with some members of the company he was touring with – they were doing J. M. Barrie's *Dear Brutus*, with which he was on tour. He took me down the valley to tea at Beddgelert.

Around the same time, he opened in a play called *Old Acquaintance* by John Van Druten, playing opposite Edith Evans.

"OLD" ACQUAINTANCE.

1941.

RUDD: "You are still magic to me, Kit."

It is the morning after all-night dancing. In the hard light of day, Kit (Edith Evans) is still entrancing to her young publisher-lover, Rudd Kendall (Ronald Ward). He tells of his hopes of a more important job. He asks her to marry him. But Kit refuses, because, she says, she is too old and their affair was never intended to be permanent anyway

GLOBE THEATRE

SHAFTESBURY AVENUE, W.1
Licensee and Manager : HAROLD GOSLING

Under the Direction of GLOBE & QUEEN'S THEATRES LTD.

MONDAYS—FRIDAYS at 2.15
SATURDAYS at 1.30 and 4.15

H. M. TENNENT LTD.

presents

"DEAR BRUTUS"

By J. M. BARRIE

Matey	...	...	...	...	...	ROGER LIVESEY
Lob	...	...	...	...	...	GEORGE HOWE
Mr. Dearth	...	...	...	...	JOHN GIELGUD
Mr. Purdie	...	...	...	...	RONALD WARD
Mr. Coade	...	...	...	LEON QUARTERMAINE
Lady Caroline	...	...	...	ZENA DARE
Mrs. Coade	...	...	...	MARY JERROLD
Mrs. Dearth	...	...	MARGARET RAWLINGS
Mrs. Purdie	...	...	NORA SWINBURNE
Joanna ...	...	...	...	URSULA JEANS
Margaret	...	...	...	MURIEL PAVLOW

Play Directed by JOHN GIELGUD
Decor by RUTH KEATING

SMOKING IS NOT PERMITTED IN THE AUDITORIUM

My diary entry for Friday, 31 January 1941:

Uncle Tony and Mum get married. Got up [from sick bed]. I wrote to her.

My letter of the same day:

Dear Mum,
 I hope you are well.
 Congraters for getting married hope you have a nice time. Thank
you very much indeed for the 5/-.

Uncle Tony was Tony Moser, a long-standing boyfriend who played the
saxophone with bands such as Geraldo and Ambrose. They parted in August
1943 and she took up with the actor Peter March, whom she'd met in Terence
Rattigan's play, *Flare Path*, during its run in Brighton.

The year went on. During the holidays, I stayed with one of the masters,
Dougal, in his house on a hill behind Caernarvon. My diary records a war that
was not going at all well. That spring, Yugoslavia and Greece were invaded by
the Germans, the battle cruiser *Hood* was sunk, British troops were surrounded
at Tobruk. But at Easter we had hot-cross buns for tea and I painted my model
Spitfire. At school I had to read the lesson in prayers and play a hymn on the
piano. I wasn't interested in my work going well or badly. I was always hoping
there would be a letter for me. And so 1941 became 1942, when something happened which altered my life and perhaps took another.
 In our small hotel rooms our beds were jammed up against each other. My
bed was by the door. I woke up one night to find the headmaster's erect penis by
my face. He tried to put my hand on it. I turned over and stayed absolutely still,
trying to breathe as though I was asleep. Eventually he went away. Another night
I was woken by a regular movement of my bed. I didn't move. I just opened my
eyes a little, but I couldn't see anything except a dark shape at the end of the bed
next to me and a low soothing voice saying something I couldn't distinguish. I
soon forgot all about this – perhaps because I was fascinated by the matron in her
tight-fitting skirt and twinset. It didn't occur to me that anything was wrong.
 During the summer holidays, Ronnie sat me down and started talking to me
very kindly and seriously. He said, 'I've been talking to Mr Carr about what's been
happening at your school. Now, I want you to be absolutely truthful, you will not
to be blamed at all for anything'. I had absolutely no idea what he was talking
about. Then he said that Richard Carr, one of my friends at school, had told his

father about the behaviour of the headmaster. Ronnie asked me if the same thing had happened with me. I told him about the night he was by my bed. 'I see. Now, you mustn't let that worry you.' I said that it didn't, but Ronnie went on, 'You won't be going back to Lake House. I think it's best for you to go to a bigger school now and I think I can get you into St John's School at Leatherhead – would you like that?' Hoping that St John's might be different, I said, 'Yes, Daddy.' I was quickly rushed off to see Captain Rivers, the bursar of St John's, who set me a sort of Common Entrance exam, in his kitchen. When he saw my answers he put them on the fire. However, it being a school for the sons of the clergy and my father being a well-known actor, I was accepted. As for my old headmaster, I learned later that the man who had paused by my bedside had killed himself.

Pat and I spent the holidays of the summer of 1942 in a house in Dorking, Surrey, that Ronnie had rented for us. It was the year of Humphrey Bogart and Ingrid Bergman appearing in *Casablanca*. We had bicycles, a cat, a Scottish housekeeper, who always wore black, and a piano. Ronnie had his radiogram brought down from London, along with his new girlfriend, Anne Firth, a very pretty blonde actress who was totally besotted with the peculiarities of Ronnie's personality but quite unable to cope with them. It was very difficult for Pat and me to have meaningful relationships with Ronnie's girlfriends; even the more serious of them weren't around long enough.

Ronnie was playing in a successful American comedy called *Junior Miss* at the Saville Theatre in London and Anne had just finished filming *The First of the Few* with Leslie Howard, who was then probably Britain's biggest male star and lived in a house with a private cinema at Westcott, just down the road. One Sunday morning as I was making my bed, I heard people coming up the steps below my window and larkily threw my bedclothes on top of them. When they untangled themselves from the sheets and blankets, laughing just as much as I was laughing, I saw that with my father and Anne was Leslie Howard. Pat and I had seen him in *Intermezzo* and *The Scarlet Pimpernel* and as the so-decent Ashley in *Gone with the Wind*. And there he was, just as if he'd just stepped out of the screen! I was at school when, in January 1943, I heard that he'd died when his plane from Lisbon to England was shot down by a German fighter (the rumour ran that Winston Churchill had also been on board).

*

One night Ronnie came home to our Dorking house – back from the show or Sunday drinks, I can't remember – and things got out of hand. He took up his familiar position in front of the fire, slightly hunched, whisky and ginger ale in one hand, a cigarette in the other, immaculate in a blue suit with gold watch chain across a double-breasted waistcoat. On the chain was a gold medal awarded to him when he was a child for saving the life of a little girl. He stood there chatting about this and that – maybe Horowitz's playing or his father's days at Eastbourne or the antics of Sid Field, his favourite comedian. Pat, Anne and I were laughing wildly as he acted out a point. But then he suddenly said to me, 'What are you laughing at? You have no idea what I'm talking about.'

'Don't be silly, Ronnie, of course he has,' Anne said, trying to avoid a scene developing.

'Of course he has,' Ronnie said, mimicking her. 'And what the bloody hell do you know about it?'

'Sorry – I was only trying to help,' Anne said.

'Only trying to help, eh?' replied Ronnie – and went on, 'You sit there, thinking that you know how you can help, but let me tell you that you haven't the faintest idea what I'm talking about and what's more never will.' Anne looked across the room at me and Ronnie said, 'And what's that for?'

Anne asked, 'What's what for?'

'Oh, don't think I don't know,' Ronnie said, having another swallow of his whisky. 'Oh, yes – I know all right.'

And Anne replied, 'Darling – please don't spoil the evening. You know we all love you.'

'Hmm – all love me – my arse,' Ronnie said.

Eventually Pat and I, trying not to upset Ronnie any further, left the room to go to bed, with Ronnie saying how sorry he was if we should ever have to experience the things that he had to go through. I slept, exhausted, not even caring what it was all about.

My new school, St John's, had an atmosphere designed to put the fear of God into any new boy. The tiled floors in the entrance hall echoed your footsteps with a heart-freezing sound that suggested there was no escape. Except in the masters' rooms, there was not a carpet to be seen. The arched cloisters that led round the quadrangle to our 'dayrooms' were cold, windy and wet in the winter and cool and shadowy in the summer. The dayroom wooden floors were unvarnished and always dusty. The dining hall was like a cathedral. On the walls were long lists of unknown people, either captains of the school or those killed in the last war, hanging alongside huge portraits of dead founders and headmasters. The lats, as we called the lavatories, were an open-plan brick building with doorless cubicles, with no heating and with thirty-foot lengths of wood with holes every four or five feet, through which one shat into a common gutter, the pupils' turds being carried away by a continuous stream of water, which failed to remove the awful stench. We slept in iron bedsteads in unheated sixty-foot-long 'halls' with ceilings that were thirty feet high.

St John's School, Leatherhead.

My diary tells its sad story:

November 2, 1942: No post. I don't like it so far. In JTC [Junior Training Corps – prelude to Officers' Training Corps, equipped with Boer War carbines]. Have parade. Go down town and have identity card changed.

November 3: No post. No parade. Still don't like it. Not bad. Allowed out Wednesdays and Saturdays.

November 12: Study fag. Have to clean [prefect] Silk's shoes for a week.

November 19: Clean Silk's shoes for a week again.

January 9, 1943: No post. Mum rang. Go to London to see Mum. Go to Mydd [elton Square] and see Duke (Alsatian). Play records in evening. See 'For Me And My Girl'.

February 16: No post. Write Dad. Get 200 lines from Silk for fooling in dining hall.

August 15: Have an [air-raid] Alert. Saw five planes shot down over Portsmouth.

August 22: Wring up Peggy. Go over to flat for day. Peggy is in love with a nice man called Peter March, and is apparently going to divorce Tony. Pity in a way. Go and see 'Life and Death of Colonel Blimp'. VG.

There was joy to be had in between the loneliness and bewilderment. Our housemaster, Fred Murray, was a very kind man who tried hard to help me be part of the school community and I made a few friends along the way. There was a fine Broadwood grand piano in the library which we were not allowed to play but on which I had lessons from Dr Reed, our eccentric music master, who would cry, 'Look out, the Boche are coming,' when the air-raid warning sounded. The place was full of extraordinary characters. Our woman nurse had a black moustache, our matron was Scottish and impossible to understand, and our headmaster ran everywhere. As a fag, one of my duties was to make toast on a gas ring. After lunch we looked on the notice boards to see what delightful sport was in store for us. It could be football, rugby, fives, or going for cross-country runs of about four miles in length, on which, if you were caught walking, you were beaten.

On 28 February 1943, I wrote to my mother:

My Dear Chatsby,

Thank you so much for your letter which arrived on Friday evening. J.T.C. stands for Junior Training Corps, it used to be called O.T.C. which is Officers Training Corps, I think it is an awful bore, in fact playing at soldiers but still I suppose it helps us to become officers if necessary. Last Wednesday we had a junior cross country race of about 5 miles in which I got cramp in my stomach and came in 34th out of 40 – pretty grim. In J.T.C. no. 1 and two squads attacked 3 squad in maneuvers (so to spell) but we were turned out of our positions by members of a nearby convent. Yesterday the senior cross country race took what is known as place. Very exciting. Only four more weeks to end of term. Do you think I could have a few stamps. Sorry. Thank you. Oh! All my love Mike.

On a hot summer Saturday afternoon, I managed to break my neck. A few of us went swimming in Epsom. I was standing at the shallow end of the pool, full of adrenalin and very pleased with what I thought were my beautifully executed racing dives, when I saw a dark-haired girl standing in the water a few feet from me. I thought: I shall dive between her legs and lift her on to my shoulders. I dived, and hit the bottom. I managed to climb out but the back of my head was resting on my back and my throat was so taut I could hardly breath. My friends helped me dress and I boarded the double-decker bus back to school. On arrival at the school, we went into the great dining hall for tea. After one of the boys tried to click my neck back so that I could eat without choking, I gave up and went to see our nurse. As I approached along the gravel path to the sanatorium, a window rattled up and a voice rang out. 'Stay still – don't move.' I froze. She came running out and with an assistant carried me into the san and laid me out on a bed. I heard the bell of the ambulance. I was taken to Leatherhead Cottage Hospital, where I spent the night sand-bagged so that I couldn't move my head one millimetre.

Prayers were said for me in chapel and a surgeon came down from London and put me in a plaster cast from the top of my head to my waist. I was lying there, terrified to move and very hot, when the school nurse came rushing in to the ward, exclaiming, 'Your father's mad!' She came to tell me that she had phoned my father at the Saville Theatre, where she caught him just as he was going on stage to play the father in *Junior Miss*. She said to him, 'Your son has dived . . .' My father thought she had said, 'Your son has died,' and answered, 'Ah! well now – there's nothing I can do about that,' and ran down to the stage to take his cue.

That summer, my sister and I were sent down to Weston-super-Mare for the holidays to stay with Billie Statham, the sister of Ronnie's girlfriend, Anne Firth. She was married to a test pilot called Hugh, who flew the Mosquito planes he was testing low over the sands when he knew we would be on the beach. Pat and I had a wonderful holiday. We did happy things together, sauntering down the pier and across the sands, seeing films, riding bikes around the town. These scenes have a sharpness that comes out of terrible hindsight, because we were never to be together again.

4

By the end of our holiday, Pat was unwell. Nobody was quite sure why. I had to go back to school. A few weeks into the term, after I had received letters from Ronnie and Peggy saying how ill Pat was becoming, I, for a change, became interested in the biology class and I wrote this rather strange and off-hand letter to Peggy.

St John's, November 7, 1943

I have now found out exactly and definitely what is wrong with Pat – you probably know anyway – here is the explanation.

Providing that what I have heard about her (is true), her ill health is due to the marrow of the bone not producing enough haemoglobin.

This chemical forms a very important part of the red corpuscles contained in the blood. It also carries oxygen to various parts of the body, eg the muscles and so on. If the oxygen is not carried to these parts of the body they just pack up. That is why Pat is having blood transfusion so that she might use other people's haemoglobin contained in their blood.

Eventually, with complete rest and transfusions in every position, her own marrow, having been tickled up by the other people's haemoglobin, will again begin to produce this haemoglobin.

If allowed to get bad it causes death in about two months I think or longer, but I don't think Pat's got it badly at least I hope not, I know it's pretty serious though for even a slight attack of it. So there you are in what is known as a nut shell.

Well – I must now go so cheerio, Oh!

By the way I am going to Weston next hols so I shall be near Pat which is rather good.

Love to Peter – all love – Michael.

Of course I had no idea what I was talking about – I suppose I was showing off. But later I realized it was leukemia.

From Peggy's diary, 25 November 1943:

> Hospital in morning to see Pat, back to lunch, 'phone message from hospital, Pat suddenly worse calling for me. Mummy and I sat with her till the darling passed over at 3.50 pm. God Bless her. Mummy and I walked by the sea.

The news was kept from me for several days, and it was in ignorance of my sister's death that I was confirmed and baptized into the Church of England.

I remember a charming man with white hair and brows, a soft voice and enquiring eyes: he was our bishop. He said to me, 'Do you believe in God?'

I said, 'No.' There was a small pause, then I said, 'I'm sorry. I have tried.'

Undeterred, the bishop said, 'Well, it's good that you are about to be baptized. You must go on trying to believe. I can tell you that the love of God is quite wonderful and very helpful in life.'

I said nothing.

He continued, 'Tell me, Michael, why do you want to be baptized and confirmed?'

Then I plucked up courage to say that I would be getting a half-holiday.

'Oh dear,' he said, and chuckled a little. 'I'm sure you don't really mean that.'

I hadn't the heart to disillusion him any further, so I said nothing and, as I left the room, he very kindly wished me luck for the next day's ceremony.

My father's girlfriend, Anne Firth, came down in a beautiful yellow coat and everybody said how lucky I was to have such a glamorous mother (though I didn't know it, my father and my real mother were mourning the death of my sister in Weston-super-Mare). My godparents were my housemaster, Fred

Murray, my music master, Dr Reed, and Edith Evans, who was unable to be there but sent me a sweet letter and a cheque for two guineas, the first of many such cheques.

A day or two later, Fred Murray summoned me to his study. From behind his desk, he quietly said, 'I'm afraid I have to tell you, Michael, that your sister, Pat, died last Thursday. I am very sorry.'

I didn't seem to feel anything. It was as though she had been sent somewhere else for the holidays. Everybody was very kind and people told me how sad they were for me and said that although I would never forget her, I would eventually find a way of living without her. But they didn't understand that we lived without each other anyway. We never knew if we would spend the holidays together. We had no home waiting for us. So that when she died I didn't miss her as I had seen people miss each other in films. It didn't seem like that at all. I wasn't going to see her again – that's all.

How crass I must have seemed. Now I can see that my life may have been very different had she lived. Now I cry. Then I went back to the right day in my diary:

Darling Pat died at 4.30 pm. In paper. Her last words were 'This is all very confusing'. Poor darling died a painless death.

Pat.

A three-day holiday in London followed. There were visits to see Ronnie in his theatre dressing room, trips to the cinema with Peggy, dancing to the music of Carol Gibbons and the Savoy Orpheans at the Savoy Hotel and, strangely, a visit to Jack Strachey's house, where he played his song 'These Foolish Things' to us. Looking back, I can see Ronnie and Peggy were trying to protect me from grief, and I suppose it must have helped, but what they didn't know was that it wasn't necessary. Or was it?

My school career continued to be undistinguished. There were some bright moments. In August 1944 I went to 'harvest camp' somewhere in Hampshire, where we slept four to a tent and breakfasted under summer skies which all day long were filled with slow, throbbing formations of bombers on their way to France. Our work was to hoe swedes, scythe thistles, put up fences. In the evenings we cooled ourselves swimming in the river at the bottom of our field and then went off to the local pub to smoke Senior Service and drink best bitter, never quite managing the courage to chat up the Land Girls at the bar. We were so grown up, but the other boys seemed much more grown up than I. As for my education . . . here is my report for spring 1944.

Music: He is rapidly improving. L.H.B.R.

Form Master's General Report: Disappointing. His interest & progress have equally waned. J.V.H.

House Tutor's Report: No! Completely off the boil. But he is worth taking trouble over, as he has intelligence to appeal to. He won't be able always to laugh off every crisis. F.H.M.

And, finally, the headmaster

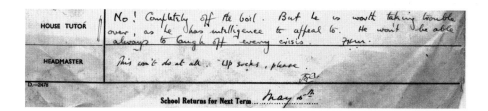

My summer report was slightly improved ('Finds things difficult, but no need for discouragement,' wrote the headmaster), but by winter I was miserable. If only I could be a weekly boarder! Ronnie had given up the house at Dorking but I thought I could go up to London at the weekends to stay with either Peggy or Ronnie. I wrote to Ronnie and kept on writing and asking if he had spoken to my housemaster about the idea.

Letter to Dad, 13 December 1944:

Thank you very much for letter and 10/-. I have talked to Doc (My music teacher) He says <u>don't</u>, if you want to take music <u>or</u> acting, stay on another term, merely because it would be a waste of valuable time.

You see I just can't concentrate on music and ordinary work at the same time. So <u>if</u> I did come back I should have to give up taking music seriously, which I definitely don't want to do. I <u>have</u> thought very carefully over this Dad, and have frankly ignored personal feelings at having to come back. And I <u>really think</u>, as Doc does, that I would benefit more by leaving than staying on. So <u>please</u> Dad, let me leave this term.

May I say that I think the world of you for being so damned nice about all this. Longing to see you Monday. All my love Mike. xxxxx.

But I had been left in the dark: my dear father had written to my housemaster three months earlier to tell him that I would be leaving the school at the end of the term. In hindsight I can see that it was probably the worst decision that he could have made for me. Perhaps he genuinely thought, despite contrary advice from the Royal Academy of Music, that I could, with hard work and total application, succeed as a pianist.

He worshipped his father, Theo, who didn't start studying music seriously until he was sixteen, but still became a fine musician. I was just fifteen and although I think I was honest and sincere in my reasoning in my letters to Ronnie, I think I knew in my heart that I would never be able to reach the summit of the mountain I was putting before me. And so it proved. Without hard work, I was simply not talented enough to achieve even modest success as an actor or a musician, and hard work was then beyond me.

My housemaster and my headmaster were appalled and both asked Ronnie to reconsider his decision. Fred Murray wrote:

A real bombshell, was your last letter. For three weeks I worked with Michael on a farm, and he is quite, quite definitely a grand chap. Like most people he meets, I am very fond of him indeed & wd hate him to leave us. But apart from that I must be obstinate, to a degree of impertinence if necessary, in trying to persuade you from taking him away. I have always appreciated his intelligence and his worth at book learning . . .

But Ronnie's mind would not be changed and, just before Christmas 1944, I left St John's for the last time. On Boxing Day I made the eight-hour train journey from London to Blackpool, where I found myself walking along the seafront with my father at eleven at night. He'd just finished his show – he was playing with Clive Brook and Nora Swinburne in *The Years Between*, which came to Wyndham's Theatre, London, where it ran for two years. Man to man with my father on Blackpool prom, I felt very grown up and intoxicated with the thought that 'freedom' lay ahead.

Back in London, I moved into a house that Ronnie had rented in Edgware, next door to a Mrs Peacock, who gave piano lessons. She was very friendly and very fat. I practised hard – repeating and repeating Chopin's Nocturne No. 2 in E flat and the first movement of Beethoven's *Pathétique* Sonata until I thought I could play them well enough to sit for the entrance exam at Trinity College of Music, London. The day came. I sat down at the piano in front of the principal, Dr Greenhouse Alt, and two other people. I was so nervous that I had no real idea what I was doing, and I must have sounded very mechanical when I played the Beethoven. Still, I heard murmurs of approval. Then I was asked to sight-read something. They didn't give me any music, so I 'sight-read' the nocturne that I knew by heart. More murmurs of approval. I was in! And not only in, but (when I later won a piano scholarship) at much reduced fees. My domestic situation was also looking up. Betty Baskcomb had returned to Ronnie's life (at the beginning of the war she had given him up and married Anthony Lehmann, but he had died fighting in Italy in 1944). Now Ronnie and a friend of Betty, Norda Macpherson, agreed to buy a house for all of us – 2a Netherhall Gardens, London NW3, just off the Finchley Road. There was a floor each for everyone, and for the first time in my life I had a room that I could call my own.

I now bicycled every day to Trinity College. Sitting among my fellow students, whose ages ranged from eleven to seventeen, in a lecture room which contained two black grand pianos, I began to realize that I was somehow not the same as those around me. I didn't speak their language and I was quite unable to understand what was going on. I was in an improvisation class. The lecturer would play part of a melody and then ask one of us to develop and harmonize it, either by singing or by playing it on the piano. Quite a few of those around me showed astonishing skill at this, especially the younger ones, but I could contribute nothing. I got on better with the one-to-one teaching of my piano tutor, a fine artist called Marguerite Wolff, who put me to work on semi-virtuoso pieces which included Chopin's *Revolutionary Study* and *Fantasie Impromptu*, Beethoven sonatas, and Brahms's rhapsodies. I gave reasonable performances of some of them at end-of-term concerts, earning praise for my interpretations, but then, in my third year, I was moved to another professor, who very quickly knew, and told me, that I was not of the material that concert pianists were normally made.

My new teacher, Henry Gheel, was a robust, round man of about seventy, with thick, untidy white hair and a Viennese childhood – he said at the age of seven he had once encountered Brahms. I walked into the practice room for my first lesson with him. He motioned to me to sit at the piano. He asked me to play for him. I played some Beethoven. He said nothing. I played some Chopin. He said, 'Play me some scales.' He then rose from his chair, put a hand on my shoulder and said, 'Give it up.' I sat silent as he explained that I had started playing much too late to enable my fingers to master the intricate work that lay ahead if, that is, I wanted to be a performing artist. However, he said, 'We can have a good year learning a few things that you will enjoy.'

This should have told me something: forget music and find something else. But I was enjoying myself too much. After the war, Trinity was full of American servicemen. I can still hear the marvellous, shattering noise made by the American band as they started the first number at the college Christmas dance, at which, dressed in my father's tails, I made a fool of myself trying to join in on my clarinet. I lived in a nice house, my dread of school was over. There were Glenn Miller, Artie Shaw and Benny Goodman to discover on records (I had a handsome blue-leather HMV gramophone, which my housemaster at St John's had helped me to buy just before I left) and girls to discover all over the place. I persuaded myself I was working, impervious to the fact that I was getting nowhere. I worked as a barman at the Players Theatre some evenings. I enjoyed the exhilaration of whizzing through the traffic on my bike, but when I was on public transport, and my inevitable erection occurred, I was obliged to bow off the bus as modestly as possible.

Into this careless blankness came my dear, sweet Mother.

Peggy, *circa* 1945.

5

I remember some details of when and how it first happened – not all, but some. After college one Saturday morning – it would be my first year – I went to the HMV shop and bought Glenn Miller's recording of 'Tuxedo Junction'. As I sauntered through the shoppers on Oxford Street, I thought, 'Peggy would love this record,' so I turned into the back streets of Soho towards Winnett Street, allegedly the shortest street in London, where my mother was living in a flat behind the Globe and Queen's theatres. Outside her flat I whistled the family whistle, which was the first bars of Beethoven's 5th Symphony. She came to the window and threw the keys down. I asked her if she could give me some lunch; I had no money and anyway it didn't occur to me to take her out – I had something to play her which I knew she would go crazy over.

She put some coffee on, made a snack and we put the record on. It transfixed us. We clapped our hands on the off beat, said things like 'Listen to that sax player, Tex Beneke,' and told each other what a great band it was. She caught my hands in hers – I thought in delight to the music and made to free them. She wouldn't free them. She looked hard into my eyes without flinching. Something was odd. She kissed me on the lips and held me there. I pushed her away, gently. She continued to look at me. I kissed her. Such a strange delight came over me. I fought hard but it was no good; it suddenly went too far. I had sex with my mother. There were joy and wonder and innocence, and then the thought, 'Christ, my mother's in love with me.'

I don't want to think about how long it went on for – a few weeks, certainly, in those last months of the war. Peggy had just turned thirty-eight and she was incredibly glamorous. I was proud to be seen with her. We shared a sense of humour. We listened to jazz together and I neglected my studies to be with her. But I was also very frightened. I tried to keep the wonderful happiness I thought I had found from being destroyed. But the innocence of a son's love for his mother had become a lust for her. What had been a lovely, open love became a horrible secret. She said I must never ever tell anyone what had happened because it was against the law. I promised that I never would.

She became incredibly jealous, and the fact that I wasn't jealous led to terrible rows – not just rows, but appalling fragments of time, fraught with tears and violence. There was an intense, unreal emotional security in the relationship which I used as an excuse not to face up to the reality of it.

I came back to the flat one night determined to end it. I walked into the bed-sitting room and sat down in the winged chair opposite the bed. She was lying on the bed in her dressing gown. She greeted me with a loving look. I looked at the chest of drawers with the photographs of my grandfather and granny on it, her parents. I thought of what they would say if they knew. I didn't know how to start. When she looked at me I knew she knew something was wrong. I suddenly started crying and she started crying. I tried to say something but fell silent. I thought I must talk to my father but I felt scared of his anger – and also his hurt, because I had come to love him. There was no one I could turn to. I knew what I had to do. I knew I must end it. It was the most terrible scene: her screams, my sobs. She grovelled on the carpet at my feet, groaning that she would do anything, if only I would stay. But I knew that if I weakened I would only have to repeat the horror of what was going on. She promised that, if I did stay just a little longer, just till tomorrow, she wouldn't cry any more. She would understand how I felt and would let me go without trying to stop me and then we could remain friends.

But I knew I couldn't trust her. I left my mother and didn't see her again for many weeks. I was profoundly scared. I couldn't be sure if it was safe to see her without invoking pitiful false hope on her part and angry recriminations on mine. But then again she was my mother. I needed to see her. Eventually I found the will to phone her and we met for coffee. We searched for a way forward. I wanted us to relate to each other as mother and son. To begin with we agreed not to meet too often. We had more coffee. We went to the cinema. She came to Trinity from working in a show in Brighton to hear me play. We met more often and soon I had lunch with her a few times a week when I was working at the college. She was actually awed by the stupidity and destructiveness of what had happened and although, in hindsight, I realize how much emotional harm I suffered over the years, there unfolded a relationship of happiness and respect between us until her death in 1990.

Partly my fear that it would not be understood and partly my promise to her not to tell anyone kept me from doing so for twenty-seven years. Eventually I found the courage to tell Elizabeth, my fifth (and final) wife. At first she was shocked and then she gave me such love by saying it wasn't my fault; I became physically lighter.

I don't think it could have happened if my sister had lived, though I am not sure why I believe that. The real question is: how *did* it happen? For Peggy, I can only guess. Did she fall in love with me because she had never known me as a son and now suddenly there I was, approaching manhood, a fond young man with similar tastes and mannerisms? But she knew I was her son and under age, so how did she allow herself to seduce me? After her marriage to Ronnie broke down, the fact is that she became extremely promiscuous, a sexually voracious woman who let few things stand in her way, even, in my case, the most ancient taboo. I can only guess this, but sex to her was perhaps a thing unto itself, unconnected to the norms of other human feelings and behaviour. As for me, I have to keep reminding myself that I was sixteen years old, and as a child I had had little of the normal, tactile tenderness of a mother to her son. There had been very little of that thing called 'bonding'. From the age of three, I didn't live with her. She wrote me affectionate letters all through my life – she was a mother on paper – but I can't remember her visiting me at school and I can think of only two occasions when she saw me in the holidays, in 1936 and again in 1937, both times with my grandparents. I was a sixteen-year-old boy afflicted with the usual adolescent sexual fantasies and longings, and I was also badly in need of some loving affection. I had no idea how to resist. Indeed, why would I resist?

6

After three years of being together and one year of marriage, Peggy was divorced from Peter March on 13 May 1946. That was the end of her third marriage; there were others to come – two more for her and five for me.

At college I fell in love with a teacher, Lettice Laird-Clowes. I watched the way she sat at the piano, the way she swayed to the phrases she was playing. A plain scarlet dress clung to her olive skin and, having reached the stillness of the end of the Brahms Intermezzo, her head inclined and she smiled a silent question. She was enchanting. She was one of the professors at Trinity College. The daughter of a naval historian, she had a widowed mother.

We went out to the country together. She wore a lime-green dress patterned with black-stalked flowers. We lay in the sun in a field near High

Lettice at 28 Holland Park Mews, *circa* 1949.

Wycombe. Little beads of sweat formed on her forehead and we hesitated. On 11 December 1948, when I was nineteen and she was twenty-seven, our hesitation ceased. Ronnie, Betty and Peggy came to the wedding in a church off Onslow Square, Kensington. We spent a honeymoon night or two at the Mitre Hotel in Oxford and then moved in to a lovely flat, 28 Holland Park Mews.

At the end of three years at college, it was now obvious that my earlier optimism about a career in music had been seriously misplaced. I had to find work. I got a job as assistant to a dear little old lady called Miss Moon, who ran the London Music Shop, above a newsagent's in Wimpole Street, around the corner from Trinity College. At the top of a flight of steep, uncarpeted stairs a door opened on to a tiny room stacked with sheet music from floor to ceiling. As you came into the room, looking for a way through the music, a small voice would say, 'Can I help you?' White-haired Miss Moon in her gold-rimmed spectacles sat behind more piles of music at a desk by the window. My job, apart from serving in the shop, was to rush all over London on my bike or (sometimes) motorbike, collecting music from publishers. The meagre pay for this job was my financial contribution to the marriage, which soon began to waver. I was a flirter, from a tradition of flirters, though on 4 March my father put a little of that behind him when he at last married Betty Baskcomb at Hampstead register office.

Eventually, in 1950, I decided to be an actor, on the grounds that if my father could do it so could I. I had no training, but managed to join the Bromley Repertory Co., where I quickly discovered that acting was not necessarily an inherited talent. I was hopelessly nervous. I didn't know how to project my voice, so that when I could remember my lines nobody could hear me. Peggy and Lettice came down to seem me play Curio in *Twelfth Night*, but I had only one line, which I think they heard, and in any case said I looked wonderful. Two women in the cast were the backbone of the company, both wildly attractive to me, and I had a delightfully light-hearted affair with one of them, Margaret Anderson, who later married Guy Verney, the company manager.

Perhaps I had the carelessness that sometimes comes with good looks – I was certainly careless of my marriage to Lettice – but the looks helped when it came to film work and in the early 1950s I began to get a few small parts in them, changing my name to Theo Ward because I discovered another Michael Ward who was having much more success than me. (Later I became Lawrence

My father and Betty Baskcomb on their wedding day.

Ward and then – oh my! – Rhett Ward.) In *Miranda*, I played a rather camp hair-dresser called Alphonse. The film was about a mermaid and I had a small scene with Margaret Rutherford and Glynis Johns. I didn't see the film until years later when it was regurgitated on television – and then, of course, my scene was cut.

On 11 May 1950 Peggy married for the fourth time. Her new husband was an actor/singer called Dennis Wood, a personable, tall, dark chap who was getting a few parts in plays outside London which just about kept them going. Peggy was very happy with Dennis until they found they had to resolve the problem of Dennis's homosexuality – a delicate predicament that they found very tricky to absorb into their lives. All three participants got on well, but the sincere efforts of two to 'cure' him, not surprisingly, failed (and were abandoned when, in 1956, Dennis went to Italy to live with his friend Ron).

At this time, my father was in a play by Kenneth Horne called *A Lady Mislaid* at the St Martin's Theatre and I had got a job at the London Coliseum after

Margaret Rutherford, Glynis Johns and MW in *Miranda*, Pinewood, 1948.

auditioning, or rather lining up, with around 200 other males who wanted £10 a week for lying about the set doing nothing in an American play called *Mr Roberts*. 'The one with the light pants' was how Joshua Logan, the director, identified me to join the cast, which meant that for the next six months I had to go under a sun lamp and cover myself in oil every day to be part of the crew of an American Liberty ship operating in the Pacific. I shared a dressing room with Charles Stapley and Roger Moore. Roger was then still almost married to the singer Dinah Shore, and at the end of our run I said to Roger that, if I didn't have a lucky break soon, I would probably give the business up. He replied, 'Oh really? I'm going to be a big star.' The cast was headed by Tyrone Power, Jackie Cooper and George Matthews, all considerable stars. Power was driven about in a black Rolls and bought himself a beautiful silver Jaguar XK120. At his Christmas party, a large two-tier chocolate and cream cake commanded the centre of the room. One of the guests, almost certainly a star but not one known to me, asked Power if he minded if he sat on the cake. Power said, 'Please do.' People gathered round to watch. The man took off his trousers and

65

underpants and ploshed down on the cake, which oozed up to cover his private parts in chocolate and cream. A cheer went up and someone took a picture. I'd never seen anything like it before, and mercifully I haven't since.

I never got to know Power, but I did become friends with George Matthews, a gentle gorilla of a man with whom I played chess between shows on matinée days. He had a remarkable sense of humour but never laughed at anything. He was always saying that if a pussy could be air-conditioned he would live in one. When the show closed I earned a little money by driving George and his air-conditioned wife around Britain. My first marriage was almost over by then – I think (no, I know) that I had no idea of how to integrate sex into a normal everyday relationship. I moved in to a flat in Harley Place with another actor, Ewan Lloyd, who had a part in a Robin Hood film being made at Denham Studios, where a few years earlier I had been too frightened to accept an offer of an apprenticeship in the cutting rooms. My agent got me the part of the thirteenth merry man. I promptly fell in love with Joan Rice, who was playing Maid Marion – one of those one-sided romances that finished before it began.

Tony Forewood, who was once married to Glynis Johns until he got his sexual outlook sorted, was playing Will Scarlet. Tony was Dirk Bogarde's boyfriend/manager. After filming had finished one evening he asked me back to dinner at Bendrose, their house near Amersham. I was a little apprehensive. I messed about on the piano and Tony said I would be great for parties (he obviously didn't know what he was talking about). It got very late – talk, talk, talk – and I was asked if I would like to stay the night. Upstairs I was about to enter my room when I was asked if I would prefer to sleep alone. I said thank you, but I would. There was no persuasion and no further invitations except to have lunch and swim at Bendrose on a couple of Sundays with the lawn full of other guests, one of whom, a beautiful American blonde called Nan with one arm in plaster, I drove home to my new room in Queen's Gate, Kensington.

To me, Forewood and Bogarde were striving to keep up the asexual film star/manager image of themselves, as though they weren't quite sure of who I was or what I represented. Tony was easy and forthcoming, though also aware of Dirk's wishes. Dirk, on the other hand, appeared shy and unapproachable; he offered himself to you through his smiling humour, but his body language said 'I'm untouchable.' For a while, I became friendly with his mother and his brother, Gareth, and I used to go shooting in the fields near Bendrose with my 2.2 rifle. But Dirk had always a sophisticated social armour around himself.

Dirk and MW by the pool at Bendrose, Amersham, *circa* 1956.

But I have stepped ahead of myself in this narrative and need to go back to 1952, when I fell in love again, this time with Gillian Lutyens, the granddaughter of the architect. But, again, I wasn't content to have an affair. I looked on her as the loveliest, dearest person I had ever met and told my diary that I loved her so much that no one else mattered. We hatched a plan to get married, which, given that I still needed to get my divorce from Lettice, pay off my debts and earn some money, needed to be a five-year plan. In the event, those five years were spent getting married to, and divorced from, another woman entirely.

One day in 1952 my agent called to ask if I would meet Bernard Vorhaus, an American director who was in Britain to escape the claws of Senator McCarthy's Un-American Activities Committee. Vorhaus was shooting a film in Italy entitled *Fanciulle di lusso* (*Finishing School*) and needed an actor to play the part of an American called Greg. My accent was appalling, but I acted my head off at the audition in the Mayfair Hotel and, to my astonishment, I was given the role.

I flew to Rome and there felt very alone. I knew nobody and not a word of Italian. I stayed in my hotel room for at least three hours before I dared pick up the telephone to order some food or coffee. The next day a car picked me up and took me through the derelict and poverty-stricken suburbs of Rome to the Cinecittà studios, where I met my American accent coach and the female star of the film, a promising young actress called Susan Stephen. In this film I was also a star, or at least I had a star part – my first and last – and she and I got to know each other. Soon I lost entire control. We made weekend trips to Naples and went to lavish parties and dinners. I changed hotels to be nearer Susan – and then changed rooms again to be nearer still. We lay in bed listening to the church clock outside our room striking a minor third in the hot sunshine. We went to the Dolomites for a couple of weeks, and on to Portofino, where we stayed at the Splendido, and then back to Rome to finish the picture.

We married on 22 November 1952, soon after we got back to England. Thanks to Susan's publicity manager, the London *Evening Standard* announced the fact on the front page. As to the film, it was never released in England because the censor took exception to a couple of lesbian scenes. I never saw it, or what turned out to be the apex of my screen career.

MW and Susan Stephen at Cinecittà studios, shooting 'Fanciulle di lusso'.

Before I entered the scene, Susan had been engaged to David Conville, an actor who later became an impresario and director in the West End and chairman of the Regent's Park Theatre Company. The ending of their engagement was amicable and after Susan and I were married we went to stay with David and other friends at his father's house in Colchester. A game of strip poker was announced. When Susan lost her bra, I heard David say that he 'hadn't seen those for a long time'. Quite a jolly evening seemed in the offing, but David was sad that his new fiancée, Maggie, was 200 miles away in Lancashire with her mother. I had a silver-blue Jaguar XK120 and gallantly resolved to fetch her. The return trip took several hours, even with dangerously fast driving, and when we got back to Colchester the strip poker was of course long over and had been replaced by a torpid, naked decadence.

Fifty years later, I rang David to tell him of Susan's death. We were reminiscing when David said, 'Susan was a sexy little thing. Do you remember that night we were playing strip poker and you suddenly said you would go off to fetch Maggie? Very soon after you left, Susan said to me, "He'll be gone for at least four hours. Come on, let's have one last go." I was flabbergasted – I pointed out that I was in love with Maggie and that she was married to you. I kept this up for what I thought was an admirable time. Then I'm afraid I weakened. I was just climbing into bed when we heard the crunch of your tyres on the gravel.'

Susan, my third wife, in *The Red Beret*

The Little Hut was playing at the Lyric Theatre with Robert Morley, David Tomlinson, Geoffrey Toone and Diane Hart, and I got the job of understudying Toone and Tomlinson. Happily, they were both very healthy. Robert Morley and Hart were not the best of friends. One night I was standing at the prompt corner as he went on stage, singing, 'If you were the only girl in the world', which was in the script, but adding in a deafening and unscripted whisper, 'you'd drive me fucking mad.' He soon learned to his horror that Binkie Beaumont, who had put the show on, was in front. There followed the usual Beaumont interview in Morley's dressing room.

In spite of my tendency to ruin our finances by buying and selling cars at a loss, we seemed very happy living in Flowers Cottage, Speen, in Buckinghamshire. It was there that Joan Collins and her first husband, Max Reed, came down to see us from London, together with the actors Jon Pertwee and Jean Marsh. The motive for their visit was an uncomfortable mixture of personal friendship and professional publicity seeking. Kurt Hutton was also there from *Picture Post* magazine to photograph a feature optimistically titled 'Love in a Cottage'. I remember being intrigued that he worked with Leica cameras, using only available light, which was pretty scarce in our old cottage.

Joan Collins, 1954.
Joan Collins and Susan, 1954.

Susan and I saw Max and Joan a bit in their London flat near Hanover Square. Once they took us on a hair-raising cruise along Oxford Street in their open Buick convertible. Max slowed at a green light on the Bond Street corner. When it turned red, he accelerated across. He called it Russian Roulette.

Clockwise from bottom: Susan, Jon Pertwee, Joan Collins, Jean Marsh, Maxwell Reed, MW. – Flowers Cottage, Speen, *circa* 1954 (photograph by Kurt Hutton, *Picture Post*).

Diana Dors and her first husband, Dennis Hamilton, had similar idiosyncrasies. We first met them when Susan was filming at Pinewood. Dennis was a happy but tragic delinquent, one consequence of which was his early death. About four o'clock one morning we were sitting behind Dors and Hamilton in their Cadillac when we came alongside a taxi rounding Hyde Park Corner. Dennis had a small searchlight mounted on his driver's door and he swivelled its powerful beam directly into the taxi driver's face. The driver shielded his eyes but Dennis persevered, and the taxi swerved about for a while before screeching to a halt. Dennis drove on, laughing. He told us he was heading for Kinnerton Mews and the home of Brian Desmond Hurst, a successful (and gay) film director. Hamilton and Dors knew that the house would be full of guardsmen. He had falsely reported a fire in Hurst's house to the fire brigade and was beside himself with joy at the sight (watched from the other side of the mews) of a puzzled Brian in his dressing gown talking to the firemen.

The 1950s are today often described as a 'grey' and 'austere' decade for Britain, the idea being that, in the poet Philip Larkin's words, sex wasn't invented until 1963. This doesn't accord with my memory of them. For example, Dors and her husband installed a two-way mirror in the guest bedroom of their house in Chelsea, so that they could watch the antics of their guests from their own room above. My knowledge of this made me suspicious of an invitation to another home of theirs in Maidenhead, a big mock-Tudor house on the river with an indoor swimming pool and God knows what else. Diana and Susan were both filming *An Alligator Named Daisy* at Pinewood. When we arrived on our first visit, Susan and I went upstairs, crept into Dors's bedroom and opened the wardrobe door. There was no back to it and we could see through a two-way mirror right into our room. We said nothing. At dinner, Dennis proudly showed off his salt cellar shaped in porcelain as an erect penis – all very daring in 1954. After dinner, we went up to our room, undressed, then turned to the mirror and, with two fingers on each hand raised in the V sign, blew them a raspberry. Not a lot was said the next morning except, from Dors, 'Ward – you're a shitbag.' Subsequently when our paths crossed occasionally, she greeted me with 'Ah – it's shitbag Ward.'

Diana Dors at Maidenhead, 1954.

In 1955 Susan went to Samoa for a film called *Pacific Destiny* (it starred a young Denholm Elliott) and I joined the rep company at the Connaught Theatre, Worthing, where I gave appalling performances and met a beautiful fellow cast member, Virginia Maskell. We had an affair but parted before Susan returned. I didn't want to leave Susan – though she, as it turned out, wanted to leave me. In the Pacific, she'd fallen in love with the film's cameraman, Nicolas Roeg, and soon after her return she and Nick came round to the flat where we'd been living (the lease on the Buckinghamshire cottage had run out) to collect her things. We had an angry row in the car park, during which I opened his car's bonnet and ripped the wires from the engine. Nick then quietly informed me that he had been a commando – information which calmed me down. (Nick himself had a temper. Ten years later he was fired from the set of *Dr Zhivago* after he told its director, David Lean, exactly what he could do with his camera.)

Virginia Maskell.

Susan had four sons with Nick Roeg, who became one of Britain's most distinguished cinematographers. Later he left her for the American actress Theresa Russell, from whom he is now separated, but all the while he kept in close touch with Susan. She died in 2000, and I met Nick at her funeral in Brighton. We were both more than seventy now and the row we'd had when Susan came to collect her things seemed very far away. We spoke quietly of her and, though we said little, it seemed hard for us to part.

After Susan left I moved into a room in Emperor's Gate, Kensington. I had a beautiful Alsatian dog, Django, and a beautiful car, a grey Gurney Nutting-bodied Rolls-Royce. I could afford neither and Django eventually had to go to new owners in the country, but I persisted with the Rolls. I loved cars, possibly more than dogs, and the Rolls gave women a misleading impression of my standing as a gentleman, which is probably how I got to know a beautiful South African model called Fay. She had long blonde hair and a soft and slightly accented voice. Quite soon, I went to live with her in her flat in Rosemoor Street, Chelsea, where it was unwise of me to agree to have dinner with her and her estranged husband – for which foolishness I received a punch on the nose.

Fay was the catalyst for a brief friendship with Stephen Ward, who was quite unable to resist impressing beautiful women with his talents, personality and his persuasive, prominently bespectacled good looks. He was a fine artist and was commissioned to draw many celebrities who later either contributed

Fay, sitting on my Rolls-Royce.

to his downfall or, fearful for their reputations, kept silent and did nothing to save him (which is also true of many of his clients who benefited from his considerable skills as an osteopath). Stephen loved to talk. He talked himself silly. In his surgery, at his portrait sittings, during and after dinner and at parties, he chatted with an enviable fluency and intelligence about the topics of the day in a beautiful baritone voice. You might say he talked himself to death.

As usual I was on the fringe of things. Stephen rented a small cottage by the River Thames on Lord Astor's Cliveden estate, where Fay and I had dinner a couple of times. I remember that we walked over to Cliveden House for a butler-served tea, a look at the paintings, an appreciation of the height of the ceilings and a wander round the swimming pool in which Christine Keeler infamously courted John Profumo, the Secretary of State for War, at a time when she was also an occasional lover of the Russian naval attaché. But when I knew Stephen that scandal was still several years away. The details of it are only too well known. Stephen got sucked into a whirlpool of fact and gossip which purported to show that he was a spy, a traitor and a pimp. He stood alone, deserted by friends and clients alike. He was charged with living off

Stephen Ward on the Cliveden Estate, 1958.

MW drawn by Stephen Ward at Cliveden Cottage.

immoral earnings – in particular, it was suggested, those of Christine Keeler and Mandy Rice-Davies. The weight of public opinion, fed by an excited press and the establishment's need for a scapegoat, became too much of a hostile fog for his innocence to penetrate. In desperation, he took his life.

By now I had a job as a runner on a film called *Uncle George* at MGM studios, Elstree. Being a runner was, I hoped, the first step to becoming a director or a cameraman. I was prepared to work my way up. But I had reckoned without the power of the film union, the ACTT. There was one other guy without a job, who as it happened didn't want a job, but he was a union member so I wasn't allowed in. Looking after the needs of actors, I discovered, was in many ways more enjoyable than acting. I looked after people as different as Wendy Hiller, Ray Milland, Charles Coburn and Athene Seyler, but they all had this one thing in common: they all, without exception, liked to show off. With some it was most endearing (Athene Seyler, for instance), with others any-thing but. I was a runner again on a film called *High Flight* where my boss was Cubby Broccoli, a sweet bear of a man who later made, with Irving Allen, the Bond movies. I was very much in love with Fay and wrote notes to her during the inevitable lulls in the procedure. During one such lull, I was listening to 'Quiet please – camera – action . . . Quiet please – quiet – lights – camera – action' again and again. Just as the director, John Guillermin, was about to say action for the fifth time, someone started talking. Bluey Hill, the first assistant, screamed out, 'QUIET – CUNT!' – a short pause and then – 'SIR!' as he saw Cubby Broccoli talking to Guillermin.

I got home one night quite late to find a pale-green Fay collapsed in an arm-chair. I couldn't wake her. I went to the bathroom to get some water and saw several empty paracetamol bottles lying on the floor. I rushed back to the living room and tried to revive her with slaps and shakings, but a few moans were the only result. I tried to force some black coffee down her throat but she wouldn't or couldn't swallow. I dashed to the bathroom and ran a cold bath. I tried to undress her to put her in the water but she was much too floppy – I couldn't get a hold on her. I dragged her to the bathroom and heaved her over the side of the bath. The water went everywhere and – a strange thought in an emergency – I worried about the people in the flat below. Fay just lay there in the water – quite still. I had to get her out. She was a great weight and very slippery. I only just managed to lever her back over the side on to the floor. I was soaking. I had to get help. Then I went through moments of deep indecision, as I wrongly or rightly thought suicide was a criminal offence. In a daze, I rang 999 for an ambulance. My life closed in on me.

Some time later there was a banging on the door and I led the ambulance men to where I had left Fay. 'Blimey,' one of them said, 'you're a bit late, Guv.' In the hospital they pumped her stomach. She started to come round quite late the next morning and I promised to marry her. She didn't answer. We were married on 2 November 1957.

We moved to 34 Cornwall Gardens, a beautiful square in Kensington, and it was there that I decided to try my luck as a photographer. My experience of photography was no more than that of the average taker of happy snaps, though I'd taken some of Fay that were used on a book jacket, and I'd had enough wit to take out my Zeiss Ikon when I saw Cary Grant and Ingrid Bergman antiques-hunting in Portobello Road market and to sell the picture to the *Evening News*.

The flat didn't have a great deal of room, but I converted the bathroom for occasional use as a darkroom, with a hinged board over the bath that could hold the developing trays. The British Grand Prix was coming up. Stirling Moss, then Britain's most celebrated racing driver, was a likely winner. I knew him slightly through the never-ending publicity appearances that my previous wife, Susan, was asked to make in the fond hope that they would further her career. Although I hadn't seen him for a while, I phoned Stirling and asked if we could meet to discuss the possibility of doing a photo story on him and his wife, Katie, during the Grand Prix. He took me to lunch at the Steering Wheel club in Mayfair and said that as long as I didn't get in his way that was fine. I thanked him very much. As I was leaving, I remembered that I didn't have a decent camera and I couldn't afford the cost of hiring one. So I went back to the table and said, 'There is one snag – I'm afraid I don't have a camera. May I borrow yours?' He had a Rolleiflex f2.8. He smiled and said, 'Yes – but mind you look after it.'

I went home and started to learn how to use it. When the Grand Prix came, I took hundreds of pictures. Stirling won, and as he was leaving the circuit he suddenly called out to me, 'Hey – can I have my camera back!'

Cary Grant and Ingrid Bergman, Portobello Road Market, 1955.

Not one of my pictures of him was ever published, but I did sell one of Katie to *Woman's Own*, biting her nails as she watched Stirling roar past the pits. It was the first time I'd taken a picture intending it for publication and had it published.

I was a photographer.

Katie Moss at the British Grand Prix, 1958.

Part Two

Fay bathing, Christmas 1958.

The first person to regularly commission and publish my photos was Peter Rawstorne, who edited an architectural magazine called *Interbuild*. He was very encouraging about my work and, as a talented designer, he made my pictures look good on the page. He was also the boyfriend of a close friend of Fay's called Patricia Arklie and we spent a Christmas together at a tiny cottage called Peakletts, somewhere in Sussex, where I took this picture of Fay:

Our marriage, of course, wasn't going well. Fay was earning good money as a model and I was earning bad money as a photographer. There were faults on both sides. I gave, or imagined I gave, everything I knew that was in my heart to my marriage, but in hindsight I can see that I was trying to manufacture domestic love; though lust was all too apparent, love wasn't visible. As to Fay, her way of getting some jobs was as old as the hills. So one night I landed on Peter's floor and stayed there until I found a room and kitchen at 29 Royal Avenue, Chelsea. (Fay and I were divorced much later, on 16 December 1962. The co-respondent, Clifford Irving, went to prison ten years later for faking an alleged 'autobiography' of the celebrated recluse, Howard Hughes.)

One of my coffee bars in the King's Road, 1958.

My new flat, at £5 a week, had everything I needed. Its balcony looked on to the gardens of Royal Avenue, I could park my Austin Seven outside the front door, and it was a marvellous base to work from. I made a darkroom in the kitchen and I wandered off for hours looking for pictures. I rarely came back with very much – rather too many pictures that were 'not quite there'.

Just round the corner from Royal Avenue, 1958.

John Piper in his studio with Coventry Cathedral window designs behind, 1959.

When I photographed John Piper in 1959, he was designing the stained-glass windows for architect Basil Spences's new Coventry Cathedral. I'd just begun to make my way as a photographer so how I landed this opportunity to photograph Piper I'm not quite sure. But Betty Frank, the ballet correspondent of the *News Chronicle*, was a great friend of my mother from their dancing days and also the girlfriend of Stanley Baron, a journalist on the *Chronicle* who had collaborated with Piper on the Shell Guides, a series of illustrated guides to the counties of Great Britain. John Betjeman was the editor who, in 1937, brought Piper on board, because he had heard that he was a keen 'church crawler'. I photographed Piper at his studio at Fawley Bottom in Oxfordshire. He was warm, helpful and patient, but somehow I couldn't relax him. Perhaps I was awed by his face – a face that guaranteed almost any picture one took of him would be successful.

I hadn't seen Dirk Bogarde for a few years and was looking forward to meeting him again. He was making the film *Libel* with Olivia de Havilland when we met on this shoot in the graveyard of St Giles's Church, South Mimms, Hertfordshire. It was fascinating to watch Asquith directing them. He had a very upper-class manner and gesticulated wildly to get his points over.

Anthony 'Puffin' Asquith directing Dirk Bogarde and Olivia de Havilland in *Libel,* 1959.

Vittorio De Sica, along with Rossellini and Visconti, was one of the pioneers of neo-realism in cinema. He agreed to let me do a few shots of him around London. We drove down to the East End, to the docks, to St Paul's and then back to the Savoy, where he insisted I take this shot of him driving my 1929 Austin Seven. I didn't have a commission and the shots were never published, but this picture at least had a small audience when it was pinned to the wall of the Savoy's press room.

Olivia de Havilland meets an autograph-hunter, South Mimms, 1959.

Vittorio De Sica in my Austin Seven, 1959.

Moment of Danger (retitled *Malaga* in the USA) starred Trevor Howard, Edmund Purdom and Dorothy Dandridge. Here the director gives instructions to Dandridge, who had shot to international fame with her eponymous role in the film *Carmen Jones* in 1954 after a long career as a nightclub performer, starting with New York's Cotton Club in 1939. In 1965, she was found dead of an overdose of anti-depressants.

Dorothy Dandridge with director László Benedek, *Moment of Danger*, 1959.

The lights were hot and the waits in between takes were long and boring – everybody seemed to be drooping on the set of *The Wreck of the Mary Deare* at MGM studios. Cooper and Heston were hanging around the set, waiting to perform in the next take; I even took a picture of Cooper asleep. Then, a magical moment – Cooper was sitting in a corner of the set and Heston moved so that he was silhouetted. The light was not strong enough to allow me to use a small aperture so that I could get both Heston and Cooper in focus and a fast enough shutter speed to avoid camera shake. Lady Luck was with me: there was a piece of scenery close to me on which I was able to lean my Leica so that I could use a slow speed, about an eighth of a second, and have my lens aperture closed right down.

Gary Cooper and Charlton Heston on set at Pinewood, 1959.

In 1959 I turned thirty. I needed to grow up. I was still having numerous one-afternoon stands, though usually in pursuit of love. Occasionally I wondered if I was trying to replace my mother, though not for long because after all, I was getting on well with her now and my sexual life was normal enough – except that it was so frequent and I kept on getting married.

Then I met a fascinating girl called Julie Hamilton, the daughter of the film maker Jill Craigie, who was married to the Labour politician Michael Foot. I didn't know it then, but Julie was on the rebound from a handsome young Scotsman called Sean Connery. We became great friends, and one Sunday we had lunch with Michael Foot and his wife in a cottage they had on Lord Beaverbrook's estate in Surrey.

Jill Craigie with Michael Foot in their cottage near Leatherhead, 1960.

Our relationship neither started nor ended in bed, which always seemed to perplex Julie. One hot afternoon she suddenly said to me, 'Why haven't we had sex together?' To which I hilariously replied, 'All right then — let's have a go now,' and we did, with disappointing results. Perhaps that's why we've maintained our lasting friendship. Later she became picture editor of *Honey* magazine and sent me off on the most wonderful jobs, such as photographing Jill Bennett and the Beatles.

Then at a party I met Tom Wiseman, who ran the Show Page on the *Evening Standard*, and he asked me if I would like to take pictures of the people he interviewed. I said I wasn't sure that I was competent enough, but he said that was nonsense. And so started five years doing pictures for the *Evening Standard*. As I wasn't on the staff, I had to do my own processing and printing. After the shoot, I'd hurry home to the bathroom of my flat in Chelsea, where I'd process the film, print some contact sheets, and from them select and caption and catalogue the prints. It took about four to five hours, so if the shooting session started in the evening, I would very often not finish printing till around four in the morning. Then — up the next morning to take the prints round to the *Evening Standard* picture desk.

I was able to do all this, because I learned so much from a very clever and original photographer, David Hurn, who had covered the uprising in Hungary in 1956 and later became a Magnum photographer. We had a mutual admiration for Cartier-Bresson and used to go off together and be 'street photographers', covering events such as the Aldermaston March. I owed David a lot.

In 1959, while I was doing a story on Tubby Clayton, founder of TocH and a former vicar of All Hallows-by-the Tower, I came across a group of about twenty Americans, and in particular an American girl, Ronnie La Roche (a cousin of the film star Rosalind Russell), who were helping out with things like Meals on Wheels and psychiatric rehabilitation, and contributing to the welfare of children who had lost their families during the London Blitz. This group was called the Winant Volunteers, after a wartime US ambassador to Britain.

Prayer time at Lady Gomm House, Bermondsey, one of the day centres where the Winant Volunteers cared for children, 1959.

Shirley Ann Field, 1959.

Shirley Ann Field was twenty-one when I photographed her. She'd just finished shooting in Michael Powell's film *Peeping Tom* and went on to great success
with Laurence Olivier in *The Entertainer* and Albert Finney in *Saturday Night and
Sunday Morning*. I was seeing her home after a session of mostly leggy shots of her
when I saw this great face through the windscreen of my Austin Seven.

I was still living a carefree life in Royal Avenue – not having the remotest idea how to pay next month's rent. In a coffee bar on the King's Road I would sometimes meet Katie Moss, Stirling's wife. There was a slight flirtation going on with Katie, quite meaningless but a flirtation nevertheless. One day she asked me to spend the weekend in Paris with her. I said I had no money for the fare. That didn't seem to be a problem. Then she asked if I would mind if she took a friend as a chaperone. The friend was a handsome brunette, Margot Beaubien, a French Canadian. We arrived in Paris, me thinking I was going to have a romantic weekend with Katie and heedless of what poor Margot was going to do. We came to the top of a Metro escalator and Katie fell into the arms of a young, very talented racing driver. Margot looked at me, a trifle sheeepishly – we never saw them again.

This was the beginning of a delightful relationship that started with three days in the bedroom of a Paris hotel. For a few months we enjoyed each other enormously. She was, relatively speaking – that is, relative to me – very rich. We went for walks with my cocker spaniel. We went to motor-racing meetings. We drove down to Bournemouth. My grandfather Harold enchanted her and Harold was enchanted in return. She made a gallant attempt to file my negatives and prints. We even began to meet her ex-boyfriends. Then one day she found a maisonette in Gloucester Place at £10 a week, which resulted somehow in my taking the flat and her moving into the Cromwell Hotel in South Kensington. Our tears showed how genuinely we felt about each other as we said goodbye at London Airport. Later she married Sir Gawaine Baillie, the racing driver, car enthusiast and avid stamp collector, and she settled down in Warninglid, Sussex.

On our wanderings about Paris I took a few pictures:

Margot Beaubien,
1959.

Man skipping, Paris,
1959.

Gendarmerie, Paris,
1959.

In 1959 my mother turned fifty-two, but she was still dancing. In April that year, while working in the South of France for Betty Frank at Le Lavendou, she met a young man called Amos, whom she described in her diary as 'the darling of my life'. Amos, charming enough, was more than twenty years younger, with a strong young body, and probably quite able to cope. He proposed to her in June but, mercifully, she passed on that one. But they struggled on in their paradise, in a cottage in Angoulême, and later in Peggy's flat in Soho, until the relationship slowly gave way to their age difference. In February 1961 Amos married another.

One morning, after having had coffee with Peggy at her flat in Winnett Street, I was wandering down Old Compton Street, Soho, and there on a lamp-post was a picture – the *Evening News* had Errol Flynn's death as its lead story and just above the billpost a salutary sign.

Time and the parking laws
wait for no man, Soho, 1959.

By the beginning of 1960 I was the owner of a Rolls Bentley, a Rolls-Royce, an Austin Seven and two dogs. I had no money but I lived in Gloucester Place, near Selfridges, in a flat with six rooms and access to the roof. I let three rooms, which left me with a spare room, a sitting room/studio, a darkroom and bedroom. I had free parking space outside my front door, and my landlords, the National Deaf Children's Society, allowed me to house my grand piano in a room on the ground floor. I was lucky. In the last few days of 1959 I'd photographed Dizzy Gillespie, Olivia de Havilland, Peggy Cummins, Bob Monkhouse, Lili Palmer, Cliff Richard — and a woman who eleven years later was to become my final wife. This was, and is, Elizabeth Seal: singer, dancer, actress, with a string of West End successes behind her (*The Pajama Game, Camino Real, Damn Yankees*) which had convinced the impresario Binkie Beaumont to

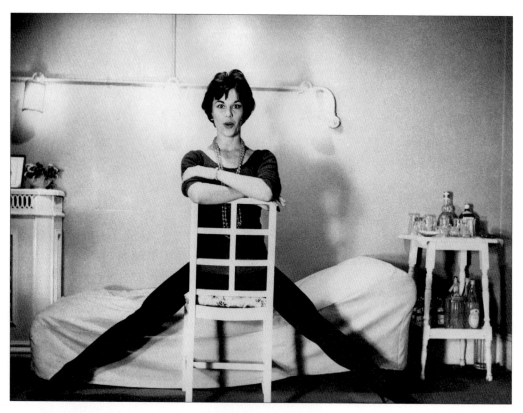

Elizabeth Seal in her dressing room at the Lyric, 1959.

Elizabeth Seal after lunch, Longcroft, 1960.

cast her as the lead in *Irma La Douce*. Peter Brook, the director, had reservations about Elizabeth but soon got over them, and when *Irma* opened in 1958 Elizabeth took London by storm (she similarly conquered Broadway when the musical transferred, winning a Tony award for best actress in a musical).

I knew very little of all this when I went along to the Lyric in Shaftesbury Avenue to meet her. To me she was just another girl/star to be photographed, processed and printed to the deadline as I struggled at Gloucester Place to pay my rent and my overdraft. But in her dressing room she made an immediate and overwhelming impression. She had a knee-weakening smile. When she asked me what we should do for the picture, I realized I hadn't the faintest idea. Later, walking down Windmill Street from the stage door, she started flirting with me. 'Quite ridiculous,' I said rather ungallantly. 'You're much too rich, much too involved and much too big a star for me to handle.' She said, 'Oh, you're so young,' and I thought, 'Christ – I'm so unsophisticated.'

The pictures, apart from the one in the *Evening Standard*, were hardly seen. I had no idea where to place them; I didn't belong to an agency. I was much too anxious trying to take pictures to worry about what happened to them.

I left my flat one shining Sunday morning in May 1960 with what can only be described as a spring in my step. Elizabeth Seal had asked me to do some photographs for her. Incredible. Quite marvellous. The venue was Longcroft, a large thatched cottage in Stocking Pelham, Hertfordshire, where we were to have lunch. Others there were the sculptor John W. Mills and his wife Jo, Clive Revill from the cast of *Irma*, and Elizabeth's then husband, Peter Townsend (no relation of the Group Captain of the same name who was in love with Princess Margaret). After lunch, Elizabeth went to sleep. When she woke we did a lot of pictures, eleven rolls of black and white and a whole lot of colour.

The first girlfriend to move in to my Gloucester Place flat was Yu Ling, from Malaya. But we soon began to antagonize each other. She left under a slight financial cloud, with me owing her some money. Not a lot, but enough for her to enlist her friend Malcolm MacDonald, the diplomat son of Ramsay MacDonald, to write to me. I paid her back when I had it.

Yu Ling, 1960.

HER DAY, said the *Mirror*. SUNSHINE BRIDE, said the *Mail*. WHAT A NIGHT —
CLARENCE HOUSE MOBBED, said the *Express*. It was 6 May 1960, Princess
Margaret was marrying Tony Armstrong-Jones, and the crowds had turned
out in their thousands to express their relief that Margaret was at last to be
happily married. In fact, Clarence House wasn't mobbed, but the joy, expec-
tation and hope were there and hundreds slept outside Buckingham Palace all
night to see and cheer and almost will that hope into reality. They had a marvellous time.

Waiting for a marriage, the Mall, May 1960.

Jacqui Chan — an exquisitely delicate woman, like bone china — was very friendly with Tony Armstrong-Jones before his marriage into royalty, and quite friendly with me.

Jacqui Chan, 1960.

In 1945 my father, Ronald Ward, was in a play called *The Years Between* by Daphne du Maurier, with Clive Brook and Nora Swinburne at Wyndham's Theatre. His dressing-room window backed on to the dressing-room windows of the New Theatre, just across the alley. One hot matinée, with the gallery stools on the pavement below full of people waiting to see Laurence Olivier in Sheridan's *The Critic*, Olivier and Ronnie caught sight of each other doing their make-up. I witnessed what happened next.

Ronnie leaned out and said, 'And how are you?'

Olivier replied, 'Most well, thank you. Tell me, do you say the same lines each night?'

Ronnie said, 'Indeed I do, especially when I remember them.'

'Ah!' replied Olivier. 'That's most gratifying – I only repeat them when I know which play I'm in.'

As the banter went on, the gallery people swivelled their heads from window to window. Finally the call boy called, 'Fifteen minutes please,' and a piece of street theatre came to an end.

In October 1960 Lionel Bart's musical *Oliver!* started its 2,618-performance run at the New Theatre and, as I went up the stairs to Georgia Brown's dressing room, I thought of the scene I had witnessed fifteen years earlier between Olivier and my father.

The paper wanted both Lionel and Georgia in the same picture and double-portraits can be tricky for a photographer. They solved the problem for me by chatting themselves into a right angle.

Lionel Bart and Georgia Brown at the New Theatre, 1960.

Billie Whitelaw, Pinewood, 1960.

I photographed Billie Whitelaw at Pinewood during the filming of *No Love for Johnny*. I left the set with her to drape her all over her dressing room, looking for a sexy shot. A total waste of time – she didn't need a body, it was all in her face.

114

Frederick George Peter Ingle-Finch, also known as Finchie, was at Pinewood too, playing in *No Love for Johnny* opposite Billie Whitelaw. Finch was a superb actor and a great womanizer – he was publicized as being friendly with Vivien Leigh, Kay Kendall and Mai Zetterling. He also romanced my second wife, Susan Stephen. A couple of years later, there was an occasion when, at three in the morning, he walked into the London flat of an American B-picture star, whose charms I had just finished enjoying. We all had coffee together. He had three wives and four children and suffered an early death from a heart attack, aged sixty-one. He is buried in Hollywood Forever Cemetery, where his neighbour is Rudolph Valentino.

Peter Finch, Pinewood, 1960.

I was inattentively watching *Armchair Theatre* one night on television when quite unexpectedly my stepmother, Betty Baskcomb, appeared, playing Janet Munro's mother. This made me sit up and take notice. I didn't care for the play very much – I remember it was by Robert Muller, directed by Philip Saville – but there was a quality about Janet Munro. She went on to star in Disney films such as *Darby O'Gill and the Little People* and *Swiss Family Robinson*. She had a sad life – two failed marriages, two miscarriages, alcohol. She was only thirty-eight when she died, choking while drinking a cup of tea.

Janet Munro, London, circa 1960.

116

I went to the Grosvenor House Hotel in Park Lane to photograph Joan Collins, who had just become engaged to Warren Beatty, which, I imagine, was why I was there. They never did marry.

Engaged: Joan Collins and Warren Beatty at the Grosvenor House Hotel, 1960.

Jill Bennett, I had heard, was a fascinating soul, but when I went to photograph her for *Honey* magazine in 1960 I didn't find much about her particularly fascinating except her face, which had a singular beauty. I photographed her again in 1971, when she was in a play by her husband, John Osborne, called *West of Suez* with Ralph Richardson. And again in 1972, in an adaptation by John Osborne of Ibsen's *Hedda Gabler* with Denholm Elliott at the Royal Court. Her remarkable features made photographing her so easy and a joy. She killed herself in 1990 after having arranged a party for her friends, knowing that she would be dead when they arrived.

Jill Bennett, London, 1960.

In October 1942, just before my first term at St John's School, Leatherhead, I was keeping a sort of scrapbook. Somebody gave me a copy of *Picture Post*, saying, 'There's a picture of your dad in there. He's being murdered!' There was also a picture of a young pop-eyed Richard Attenborough on the same page. They were both at the Piccadilly Theatre in *The Little Foxes* by Lillian Hellman. I met Attenborough eighteen years later when I went to his house in Richmond to photograph him and his family for the British Lion film company. He was then a Mr. In 1976 he became a Sir. When I last photographed him, in 1990, he was a Lord. I was still only a Michael and I doubt if he knew who I was, but he spoke to me very warmly, as though I was among his best friends.

Richard Attenborough, Richmond, 1960.

One of Peter Hall's first ventures as the new director of the Royal Shakespeare Company was to direct his wife, Leslie Caron, in Jean Giraudoux's *Ondine*. This shot is on the stage of the Shakespeare Memorial Theatre at Stratford.

Leslie Caron and Peter Hall, 1961.

At my flat in Gloucester Place I rented the spare rooms to a rich mixture of tenants who became friends and friends who became tenants. One of them was Carmen Monroe, a Jamaican girl who worked as my secretary.

Carmen Monroe with Peggy the Austin Seven.

Carmen answered a call from the *Evening Standard* one morning, and I set off to photograph Diane Cilento – it was just before she made *Tom Jones*, for which she won an Oscar nomination, just before she married Sean Connery. Cilento was very exciting – she had beautiful clear eyes and a very knowing expression. But what she knew was her secret.

Diane Cilento, 1961.

Lord Chatsby of Chelsea, Royal Avenue, Chelsea.

Dogs: in the course of my life I've had three Alsatians, three cocker spaniels, one black Labrador, one golden retriever and one Welsh Border collie. Now I have none. One of my projects when I was living in Chelsea was to do a photo story of Lord Chatsby, the first of my cocker spaniels. It never came to anything. This was one of the pictures.

I never found out whether Deborah Kerr was, with the exception of *From Here to Eternity*, in which she played an upper-class nymphomaniac, as forbiddingly ladylike as her roles suggested. When I met her in 1961 at Shepperton Studios, where she was playing the governess in the film of Henry James's story *The Innocents*, she was so glamorous and formidable as to almost deny me speech.

Deborah Kerr, 1961.

I hadn't seen Dors since the middle 1950s. In the early 1960s she was now wearing a wig for her performances, and she looked prettier than I had ever seen her – almost living up to her tag as 'Britain's answer to Marilyn Monroe'. But if she was the answer, what was the question? There wasn't an answer to Marilyn Monroe and Dors knew it, and never even considered a competition. She was doing a splendid cabaret on the top floor of a department store in Ilford and being a great success. But it was hardly a Monroe venue.

Diana Dors, Ilford, 1961.

I photographed Susannah York in the King's Road and made her dash in and out of antiques shops, and in and out of baths standing on the pavement outside the antiques shops, and then took a few shots on her balcony. She was only nineteen but already on her way to stardom with the films *Tunes of Glory* and *The Greengage Summer*. Her roles were often adolescent girls awakening to their sexuality. In 1968 I bought a beautiful green drop-head Rolls Bentley from her. It was not long before the Bentley had to be sold. It went to Australia. I've not seen her or the Bentley since.

Susannah York, Chelsea, 1961.

126

Summer 1961: I went down to Kent to photograph Peter Sellers, who was filming with the French actress Dany Robin in *The Waltz of the Toreadors*. The picture
desk asked for him in costume, but he wasn't in costume and he wasn't filming. But this turned out to be another of those occasions when the
photographer enjoys an unexpected intimacy – for about half an hour. They
were both very helpful and came out for me on one of their days off filming.
Sellers, a passionate amateur photographer, brought his Hasselblad and
Rolleiflex along and joined in. The next time I encountered him, so to speak,
was at his funeral in Golders Green in 1980.

Dany Robin and Peter Sellers, somewhere in Kent, 1961.

27 September 1961: The Modern Jazz Quartet were playing at the Royal Festival Hall – Percy Heath on bass, Connie Kay on drums, Milt Jackson on vibraphone and John Lewis on piano. I was with Peggy and a beautiful black singer called Billie Lane, who was renting a room in my flat. We sat on the stage in seats that made up a semicircle behind the players, so that we faced the audience and the MJQ had their backs to us, except for John Lewis, who sat at the piano. He played a full concert grand Steinway and Percy Heath's head and the top of his bass fiddle peeped above the open lid. Connie Kay surrounded by drums and cymbals, sat in front of us, and on the left was Milt Jackson, crouched over his vibraphone. Past them you could see, hear and feel the buzz of anticipation from the audience as they waited to hear the MJQ – live.

When the lights were dimmed, two broadening shafts of light spotlighted the players. I had to take this picture. As I raised my Leica, a uniform started waving its hand at me. I took three shots and put the camera away before the attendant could chuck me out. It was a wonderful concert and I had the mad notion to go backstage and meet them. We did – stage-door security was much less of a problem then – and they were most polite. Then – another mad notion – we asked them back to my flat for a drink. They said yes and thank you and took the directions and telephone number, but I never expected to see them again. None the less, we bought whisky and wine and asked other friends and started to have a party anyway. There were about twenty of us drinking and dancing; the joint was swinging and Peggy was having a ball, but by 10.30 there was no sign of the MJQ. Nobody cared. Then half an hour later three of them (no sign of the pianist Lewis) came up the stairs with some startlingly attractive companions, whose appearance told us that the jazzmen had come across some new friends in Mayfair.

The MJQ at the Royal Festival Hall, 1961.

January 1962: I introduced Peggy to the publicity lady at the Carlton Tower Hotel and during the year she earned a little money baby-sitting for the guests. An extraordinary job for her, because she so disliked children. My girlfriend Yu Ling, Peggy and I had a lot of dinners, lunches and coffees together, but Yu Ling and I found we had too much to fight about and eventually parted. I did sometimes wonder how much Peggy had to do with my break-ups. She was fifty-four that year but looked thirty. Also, she was a fairly constant presence in my life. I'd often take girlfriends to the Establishment Club to hear Dudley Moore playing and sometimes Peggy walked down from the other end of Old Compton Street to join us. I think I was an innocent soul. Peggy's diary entry for October 20: 'Happy day, eating, laughing and TV!'

Ursula Andress was a sensation that year – thanks to the scene in *Dr No* when she came straight out of the sea like Venus and up the beach and into the arms of Sean Connery. I took this picture of her at the Dorchester Hotel on a job for the *Evening Standard*. Her figure and composure took my breath away.

Ursula Andress, the Dorchester, 1962.

Terry and Faith King ran a rep company in Slough in the late 1940s and early 1950s, and my mother seemed to have known them for ever. For a while around that time I worked in their box office, while my mother appeared on their stage. Terry always called her by her maiden name, Willoughby. In 1962 Willoughby and I went to visit the Kings in Attleborough, Norfolk, where, from Victoria Cottage, Terry ran his antiques business. One afternoon I went upstairs to go to the loo, opened the door of the wrong room and there was Terry's son, Sean, asleep on a bed. I took a picture.

More than thirty years later, after Peggy died, Terry was speaking fondly of her when he said that in his opinion she had been the biggest influence in my life and that my wife, Elizabeth, was the only person who'd been able to stand up to her. Was I innocent or was I stupid or was I repressed? The fact is that it was not until that moment, when I was sixty-four, that I realized the truth of what Terry said. And that – perhaps – both my relationships with women and my images of them were part of a long, subconscious attempt to free myself from her.

Boy on a Bed, Attleborough, 1962.

Julie Christie,
London, 1962.

This picture was taken in the first of three sessions I had with Julie Christie –
the other two were in 1963 and 1964. She lived in a flat in west London with a
cat and was doing a film, or was about to do a film, called *Crooks Anonymous*. She
was so easy to be with and I found that I could hardly take a shot that wasn't
worth printing.

I photographed Barbara Windsor in August 1962, the year she appeared in the film of Joan Littlewood's play *Sparrows Can't Sing*. She was twenty-five and fully formed in the cheerful, boisterous sexuality that would later see her so successfully through so many *Carry On* films. We did a lot of shots, drank a lot of coffee and had a lot of laughs. The man in the picture is Gerry Garrett, who'd taken over the *Standard*'s Show Page from Tom Wiseman. Garrett was man of passionate likes and dislikes, not all of them evident in the photograph. He hated – violently – drivers who drove with dipped headlights during the day, and he was mad about the music of Gluck.

Barbara Windsor with, left,
Gerry Garrett, London,
1962.

To Shepperton again, this time to photograph Susan Hayward, who was on set for a remake of *Dark Victory*, in the part made famous by Bette Davis in 1939. When I arrived they were shooting a ballroom sequence in which Hayward was doing a tango with Jerry Desmonde, Sid Field's feed. Memories of going to the theatre with my father to see Sid Field in *Piccadilly Hayride* at the Prince of Wales sprang to my mind.

Field was so funny. In one sketch he played a photographer who was taking pictures of a town mayor (Desmonde). After a series of hysterical blunders trying to arrange the mayor's position, Field said, from under the photographer's cloth, 'Marvellous – come and have a look.' I've used the line often to make people laugh – sometimes it worked!

Susan Hayward, Shepperton, 1962.

Another picture for the *Evening Standard*, and one that I liked very much. It was taken at Geraldine McEwan's flat at Ennismore Gardens, Kensington.

Geraldine McEwan, London, 1962.

Another day at Pinewood studios to photograph Edie Adams. She was playing in *Call Me Bwana* — and when I walked on the set I was delighted to discover that Bob Hope was Bwana. I did some shots of Edie Adams, but the one the paper used was of Hope holding up a pair of knickers — presumably hers. I liked this one of Hope at the side of the set, waiting to be called.

Bob Hope at Pinewood, 1962.

I was still with Susan Stephen, some time in 1953, when I met Jackie Collins. We went with her sister Joan to lunch at their parents' large mansion flat overlooking Regent's Park. Jackie must have been twelve or thirteen. By the time I took pictures of her for the *Evening Standard* in 1963, she was twenty-two, married, and about to get divorced. She was still floundering in the starlet market – it would be another five or six years before she turned to writing raunchy bestsellers. We had lunch at a posh restaurant I couldn't afford and all through lunch I wondered how I was going to get a good picture of her. Unlike her sister Joan, she was not naturally photogenic. A very striking angular face and beautiful searching eyes, which seemed to be pleading that she was really very beautiful. Lady luck was with me and she ordered around eighty prints.

Jackie Collins, London, 1963.

Extract from my diary, February 1963:

Wednesday, Feb 20
Liverpool. Miles: 241 – Cash Petrol – £3 0s 11d Hotel – 15s 0d.

Thursday, Feb 21
Liverpool. The Beatles – Honey Mag. Miles: 67 – Cash Petrol £3 9s 6d.
Coventry. Photocall – 'See You Inside' Show. Hotel £2 10s 6d. Drinks 7s 6d.
Garage (parking) 10s 0d.

Friday, Feb 22
Return from Coventry. Miles: 147.

I drove up to Liverpool in my 1938 drop-head Rolls Bentley. I loved jazz but I didn't like pop music and I had no idea why *Honey* magazine should want to send me all that way to photograph a group called the Beatles.

McCartney and Lennon, the Cavern, Liverpool, 1963.

Beatles at the Liverpool dockside, with Lennon as usual looking elsewhere, 1963.

I met them in a pub and they looked as though they were still at school. We rushed about Liverpool taking pictures. They were very helpful as I tried to think of shots to do — except Lennon, who seemed very bored and kept looking away as I tried to line up a picture. In the evening I went to the Cavern club for more shots. I can't remember a note of what they played. I gave the pictures to *Honey* magazine and lost the negs. In 1964, the Beatles' welcome-home at Heathrow from their American tour made headlines and even I could see that they were phenomenal. Only then did I desperately search for — and eventually find — the Liverpool negatives. The cheques are still coming in.

In 1963 Peggy started working part-time at Swan and Edgar, the department store on Piccadilly Circus. In July I moved to Richmond, to a house I'd bought in partnership with a painter, Austin Davies, known as Ozzie and once, in their Liverpool days, married to the writer Beryl Bainbridge. The idea was that Austin and I would divide the house into two flats. Austin and his half sister would share the top flat and I would share the bottom one with Carmen Monroe and her son, Gregory. But (but — such a small word for such a large complication!) the situation became immediately fraught because I'd forgotten that I'd already asked someone else to marry me: Austin's half sister, a young actress Stephanie Beaumont, who'd shared some of my life in my flat at Gloucester Place.

Stephanie Beaumont at Gloucester Place, 1961.

In theory, then, I was marrying Stephanie. In fact, I was setting up house with Carmen, assuming (for some reason) that Stephanie would be happy to live upstairs with Austin. Even now I shudder at the mess I was capable of making of other people's lives. Today Stephanie and I somehow still manage to acknowledge each other.

It was about this time that I took Carmen down to Bournemouth to meet my Willoughby grandparents. I was a little apprehensive about how Harold would react to a black woman, but as soon as I opened the car door there were Harold, Granny and Peggy waiting to welcome us. Harold made a deep bow and said in ringing tones, 'Your royal duskiness'. There was a lot of laughter then, and in general with Carmen, but the relationship faltered and after a year or so Carmen and Greg were off – and Peggy took over the secretarial work that Carmen had done for me.

Rosa Dolores Averio was born in 1932 on a farm in Humacao, Puerto Rico. When I photographed her, in 1963, she had become Rita Moreno. In between she had travelled the road of most 'ethnic' actresses – from nightclub dancer and singer to a seven-year standard contract with MGM, for which she played the usual brown-shoe-polish roles, invariably dressed in a tatty old leopard skin. Then she was offered the part of Tuptim, an Asian princess, in the film of *The King and I* with Yul Brynner and Deborah Kerr, and in 1961 got the role as Anita in *West Side Story* (her first role wearing shoes) and won an Oscar for Best Supporting Actress. But in 1963 she was living in Hampstead and earning rave reviews at the Lyric Theatre in *She Loves Me*, directed by Hal Prince.

Moreno had a remarkable career. She overcame years of discrimination – and a relationship with Marlon Brando – to become the first person to win all four of the awards for excellence in her profession: an Oscar, a Tony, an Emmy and a Grammy.

One afternoon in February, she came down to Richmond to be photographed for the *Evening Standard*.

Rita Moreno at my house in Richmond, 1963.

The film *The Servant*, directed by Joseph Losey, written by Harold Pinter and starring Dirk Bogarde and James Fox, gave Britain its first cinematic glimpse of a decadent, troubled and ambiguous sexuality. Its third star, Sarah Miles, played dumb provocation quite brilliantly. The *Standard* asked me to photograph her. We got on very well. James Fox was still looming in the amorous shadows of her life but, notwithstanding, she graciously asked if I thought we should have an affair. For once, temptation was resisted, though not easily.

Sarah Miles, London, 1963.

An extraordinary afternoon in Wimpole Street in July 1963, at the house of Dr Asher, where I had been sent to photograph his daughter Jane, presumably because she was making a film with Vincent Price from Poe's story *The Masque of the Red Death*. Instead (or as well) I found myself photographing her father French-polishing his grand piano. They were a very nice family. Jane was just seventeen but already (though I didn't know this) the girlfriend of Paul McCartney, who may well have been staying in the house at the time. My first impression was of a supremely innocent, very beautiful teenager, who rather surprised me with the confidence she displayed in front of the camera. Later she married Gerald Scarfe, who was a colleague and friend at the *Sunday Times*, and we still see each other occasionally. She has matured into an intelligent and talented actress, an astute businesswoman (Jane Asher Party Cakes) and a loyal friend.

Jane Asher, London,
1963.

Most people I photographed I knew only for a short while, and then only in the artificially friendly atmosphere which hopefully springs up between celebrity and photographer. Sometimes, maybe years later, one learns things about them and one wishes one had known them better.

Pauline Boty studied at the Wimbledon School of Art and then the Royal College of Art and is now recognized as one of the leading pioneers of the Pop Art movement. She died aged twenty-eight in heroic and tragic circumstances. Diagnosed as having cancer, she refused treatment while she was pregnant for fear of harming her child.

Pauline Boty at home, London, 1963.

I should have guessed, of course, but little did I know when I photographed her that Maggie Smith was destined to become one of the world's greatest stage and film actresses, and a Dame to boot. She was charming, but made it very clear from her bearing that there was going to be none of the 'let's make it as glamorous as possible' approach. I was there because she was giving a wonderful performance at the Queen's in *Mary, Mary* by Jean Kerr, for which she won the Variety Club Award for Best Actress.

Maggie Smith, London, 1963.

18 September 1963: As I was driving down to Pinewood to photograph Gina Lollobrigida and Ralph Richardson in the film *Woman of Straw*, directed by Basil Dearden, I thought what a highly irregular pair they made. How was I going to combine the astonishing sexual impact of Lollobrigida with the straight-backed dignity of Sir Ralph, 'a Knight of the British Theatre'. This was both Anglo-centric and snobbish of me. Richardson may have had a knighthood, but La Lollo was later awarded the Légion d'Honneur by President Mitterrand, as well as appearing on the covers of *Life* and *Time* magazines. She also became a good sculptress and a serious photographer, with two or three books to her credit.

Gina Lollobrigida with Ralph Richardson, 1963.

16 December 1963: Lynn Redgrave — a chip off the old block, but what a block! Father: Sir Michael Redgrave. Mother: Rachel Kempson. Brother: Corin Redgrave. Sister: Vanessa Redgrave.

She was twenty when I went to photograph her in her flat in Eccleston Square, Pimlico, and had just finished filming *Girl with Green Eyes* with Peter Finch. It's an odd business, being with a stranger, watching their face, looking into their eyes, laughing with them, but not really listening to a word they say. Just watching. So it's not so surprising that forty years later one has no idea what they were like.

Lynn Redgrave, London, 1963.

1964: Peggy, now fifty-seven, quit her job at Swan and Edgar with a present of a bottle of perfume and came to work for me at Richmond. She also seemed to be interested in a rather staid gentleman who worked in a bank. They had coffee and dinners together and loved going to the different jazz clubs around Soho. His name was Charles de la Cruz. He became her fifth and ultimate husband, to be discarded when she discovered he didn't share her voracious physical appetite.

In May I went to Birmingham, where the Rolling Stones were recording a television programme. I met them in the canteen. They were impolite and surly, but not ill-natured. No wonder, I thought, that the newspapers were asking, 'Would you let your daughter marry a Rolling Stone?' I was working for London Records, who wanted a lot of colour as well as black and white and I had no idea how I was going to win them round so that they gave me the time. I couldn't stand their music, any more than I could the Beatles' or any other pop group's. Then I thought, 'I am going to have to risk my beautiful 1938 Rolls Bentley.' It was a lovely day, so we could have the top down and I let Mick Jagger drive, with the others standing up in the back, and we went out to the country a little way. By pretending that I was fascinated by pop music and becoming someone quite foreign to myself, I managed to get some pictures.

By the end of the year they were at the top of the *New Musical Express* chart with 'Little Red Rooster'. Today they are very rich – the world's longest-surviving pop group – and their leader is now Sir Mick.

From left: Lewis Brian Hopkin-Jones (Brian Jones), William George Perks (Bill Wyman), Keith Richards, Michael Philip (Mick) Jagger and Charles Robert (Charlie) Watts. A field somewhere in the Midlands, 1964.

In 1964 Glenda Jackson had just joined the Royal Shakespeare Company and given an extraordinary performance as the assassin Charlotte Corday in Peter Brook's Theatre of Cruelty production of Peter Weiss's *Marat/Sade*. She was twenty-eight. Her film career began five years later with *Women in Love*, for which she won the first of two Oscars. She quit filming in 1992, when she became the Labour MP for Hampstead.

Glenda Jackson, London, 1964.

August 1964: From the moment she opened the door I was in love with her. I had lunch with Peggy that day and told her so. She laughed, but when she saw I was serious, she said, 'That's wonderful, darling.' I wasn't, of course, just momentarily paralysed. Talitha Pol hadn't done many films: *Village of Daughters* (in which my old girlfriend Stephanie Beaumont also played one of the daughters) and *We Shall See*. She was the daughter of the painter William Pol, the step-granddaughter of Augustus John, and became the second wife of Sir John Paul Getty. She died of a heroin overdose in July 1971.

Talitha Pol, London, 1964.

I went to see Julie Christie again when she was packing to go and film *Dr Zhivago* under the direction of David Lean. The next year she won the Best Actress Oscar for her part in John Schlesinger's *Darling*, with Dirk Bogarde.

Julie Christie, London, 1964.

When I took this photograph of Sian Phillips, she was married to Peter O'Toole and was making a film called *Young Cassidy*, which had two directors, Jack Cardiff and John Ford. Ford directed only a couple of scenes. These, and a film called *Seven Women* two years later, were the last he directed. Phillips has one of the finest faces in British theatre and cinema.

Sian Phillips, London, 1964.

February 1965: Peggy and I queued for three hours to walk past Churchill's coffin in Westminster Hall. It was very moving – a memorable moment in the nation's history. Whatever realities might be hidden by Churchill's public image, and whatever your politics (my mother was a staunch Labourite), it seemed that everybody there felt that, without him, we would not have been a free people there to say goodbye. His coffin lay alone on a dais in the middle of the hall, a soldier, head bowed, at each corner, the queue slowly walking past, four deep on either side, the silence profound.

I hadn't gone to take pictures, but I couldn't resist. As I raised my camera a voice fractured the stillness – 'No photographs' – but I clicked the shutter and then put my camera down. I didn't process the film for many weeks, much to the wrath of my agency, Rex Features, who told me that it would have been worth a lot of money, because a press rota had been imposed which allowed for only one newspaper to take a photograph, which would then be shared among the rest, leaving the world market wide open. But if money had been on my mind I'd have found it harder to take the picture.

Sir Winston Churchill lying in state, 1965.

May 1965: Groucho Marx was in town to promote his book *Memoirs of a Mangy Lover* and I went off to photograph him at his hotel. He was a small man dressed in a blazer, grey flannels and the trademark heavy glasses and dark moustache. He was with his wife, Eden, and seemed rather stiff and austere as he chatted about himself on the sofa. Accent apart, he might have been an upper-class Englishman: perhaps that was an intended effect.

Elizabeth told me that in 1959, when she was starring in *Irma*, Groucho and Montgomery Clift came to see her in her dressing room at the Lyric in Shaftesbury Avenue. Groucho told her that he wanted to produce *Irma* in New York. She had to tell him that David Merrick had already bought the rights. As he was leaving, he eyed Elizabeth up and down and said, 'Well, I mustn't keep you – much as I'd like to.'

Groucho Marx, London, 1965.

In the summer of 1949, when I was still living with Lettice at 28 Holland Park Mews and working at the London Music Shop for twinkly old Miss Moon, I missed an opportunity that might, just might, have changed the whole course of my life. My agent sent me along to Park Street, Mayfair to meet Frank Launder, who was about to direct a film based on Henry De Vere Stacpoole's novel *The Blue Lagoon*. The story is about a young boy and a girl who get stranded and grow up together on an island in a condition of near-naked innocence. I was to test for the male lead. In a nervous state I travelled to Pinewood, went through make-up, and was given a script and a sort of loincloth. Then I was led to a set which consisted of a palm tree on a large mound of sand on which was languishing a very attractive girl in a bikini. I don't remember hearing what sort of impression I made – if any. But not long after I knew that it was not quite the right one, because Donald Houston got the part.

The girl who played opposite him – and therefore would have played opposite me – was Jean Simmons. Now, up in Bradford in 1965, I was photographing her for the *Evening Standard*, filming on location for *Life at the Top*. I had an enchanting few minutes with her in a railway carriage, during which I managed not to mention our near miss on an island in Pinewood.

Jean Simmons on a train, Bradford, 1965.

14 September 1965: I drove to Bath, where Brian Forbes was directing *The Wrong Box*. I had the most wonderful array of British stars to choose from: Michael Caine, Tony Hancock, John Mills, Peter Cook and Dudley Moore, also Brian Forbes's wife, Nanette Newman. My best picture was of Tony Hancock. There is a desolation in his face, perhaps not manufactured, as he stands against the railings, cigarette in hand, waiting to be called for his scene. In June 1968, with his life ruined by alcohol, he committed suicide.

Tony Hancock, Royal Crescent, Bath, 1965.

In 1965 my old friend Julie Hamilton rang one day to ask me to lunch: she was now, she said, arts picture editor at the *Sunday Times*. This was good news and I went. After lunch she introduced me to Christopher Angeloglou, the overall picture editor, and he tried me out on a job photographing a play at the Yvonne Arnaud Theatre in Guildford. Michael Redgrave and Faith Brook were playing in *Antigone*. None of my pictures were used, but Redgrave ordered fifty prints from me. This was an inauspicious start, but I continued working for the *Sunday Times* until I retired, thirty years later.

That autumn the Liberals held their party conference in Scarborough. They were a tiny party in those days and relied a great deal on the charm of their leader, Jo Grimond. He and his wife, Laura, very kindly and with considerable trust, endured me taking pictures in their bedroom while dressing for dinner after the leader's speech on the last day of the conference. When I sent the films to the *Sunday Times* office, back came a request for more, but this time – in the bath.

The Grimonds dressing
for dinner, Scarborough,
1965.

Jo Grimond in the
conference hall,
Scarborough, 1965.

1966: Peggy married Charles de la Cruz, the bank clerk.

I was now taking pictures of subjects beyond my original range of actors, musicians and artists, but old habits die hard. When I went to see Denis Healey, Minister of Defence, at his Whitehall office I found him sitting behind his desk. I asked him to lie down. His eyebrows rose a couple of inches. I said not on the floor but on the chaise longue, underneath one of his favourite pictures. He obliged.

Denis Healey, Minister of Defence, 1966.

Duke Ellington visited Coventry Cathedral. I was thrilled to meet a man I'd listened to with such excitement since my teens, but the Duke didn't seem equally thrilled to meet me He was dreadful: self-conscious and totally uninterested. Finally, I said, 'Just stand on the steps and look out into space.'

Duke Ellington in Coventry Cathedral, 1966.

4 February 1966: Drove to Oxford, where Elizabeth Taylor and Richard Burton were rehearsing in a school room for the University Dramatic Society's production of Marlowe's *Dr Faustus*. All very incongruous – white leather boots, alligator handbag, mink coat flung over a school chair. And afterwards, queues of autograph-collectors (the police among them), bending over so that Burton and Taylor could use their backs as a surface to write on.

Richard Burton and Elizabeth Taylor rehearsing, Oxford, 1966.

Immigration Control at London Airport, 1966.

Two viewpoints, three people seeking a resolution.

Jonathan Miller, when he was directing *Alice in Wonderland* for the BBC, 1966.

During the spring and summer of 1966 I was having an affair with a young actress, Isobel Black. The affair was passionate and physical and, much to the horror of her parents, we were engaged for a short time. I was thirty-seven, I had no children (or none that I knew of), and there was a kind of desperation in my thunderstorms of romance. Inevitably, the relationship foundered, and I went to Spain for four weeks.

Isobel Black, London, 1966.

21 October 1966: I was driving back to the office from Pontypool, having finished a story on unemployment for the *Sunday Times*, when the programme on the radio was interrupted by news of a landslip about twenty miles away at a small village called Aberfan. An old coal tip had slipped and buried the village school. The time was 9.10 a.m. and it was feared that the children were in school. The reports got worse and worse. I turned the car round and reached Aberfan in the middle of the afternoon. I could see a black scar slashed across the village on the other side of the valley. Aproned women stood in the doorways of the grey Victorian terraces, watching police cars, ambulances and the lorries that were ferrying away ton after ton of slurry – the road was black with it. Underneath many more tons lay the village school. It was like walking on deep black snow.

Teams of men, many of them miners, worked through the night with shovels and pickaxes: the noise of fathers searching for their children, the dull thud of pickaxes, the scraping of shovels, the racket of generators that were providing the light. Then a whistle would be blown to demand absolute silence, as the men strained to hear any sound that might suggest life. Usually, nothing. The desperate commotion continued all night and the next morning. There was very little mercy: 144 people, 116 of them children, died, buried alive.

Fathers searching for their children, Aberfan, 1966.

Prime Minister Harold Wilson on holiday on the Scilly Isles, 1966.

1967: Early that year my friend and fellow photographer Neil Libbert made what turned out to be an important phone call. He rang to ask me to join him for dinner with a woman he'd just met. I asked Neil why he needed me and he said that she was the daughter of a princess – he was nervous. I went along and met Lisa Heseltine, who was both very attractive and very intelligent – an intelligence that later came between us. Soon after our dinner she brought her suitcases round. By early April we were honeymooning with our Silver Dawn Rolls (on its seventeenth hire-purchase payment) in the South of France. I remember we had a monumental row the day before we went on this honeymoon, which should, I suppose, have been a portent, but we went bravely on.

It was Lisa's second marriage and my fourth. There didn't seem anything strange about it. I could justify and rationalize my record. My first marriage to Lettice fell apart because I was simply too young. My second wife, Susan Stephen, left me. And I left my third wife, Fay, because she left me without moving out, so to speak. So it didn't seem unreasonable, five years after the last divorce, to marry again.

We married on 1 April at Sheen Lane register office in Richmond, with my first editor, Peter Rawstorne, as our best man. There was champagne, cider and whisky, and we left our friends, neighbours and relatives eating and drinking as we set off in our Rolls for Lydd Airport, which in those days had planes which ferried cars to Le Touquet. First night at Montreuil: sixteenth-century hotel, cobbled courtyard, dinner by a log fire. Then onwards to the Villa Maria at Le Rouret, where we went for wonderful drives along the Corniche and I polished the Rolls for a day and a half. Next to Geneva, to stay with Lisa's mother, Natalia. We all got very drunk. I went out and pissed on the near-side wheel of the Rolls. And then home.

Lisa had majored in biochemistry and physiology at McGill University and worked for the BBC on their current affairs programme *Panorama*. Her grandfather was the English composer Peter Warlock (born Philip Heseltine) and her mother was Princess Natalia Gallitzin, the daughter of Prince Boris Gallitzin, who was shot crossing a swamp during the Russian Civil War and whose forebears commissioned string quartets from Beethoven. His wife, Maria Carlow, Lisa's grandmother, also known as Merika, was the daughter of George, Duke of Mecklenburg-Strelitz. She later married Count Vladimir Kleinmichael, known as Vanya, whose great-grandfather was honoured for making a railway in a straight line from Moscow to St Petersburg.

I had married a highly educated girl of distinguished pedigree, with no music-hall turns in her lineage. We moved in to an old farmhouse at Russell's Water near Henley-on-Thames. It was here that we had two lovely daughters, Sam and Tasha, and more monumentals.

The day before the wedding day.

and overleaf:

The wedding day.

The honeymoon.

16 March 1966: Once more to Pinewood studios – to the set of *The Billion Dollar Brain*, in which Michael Caine was starring, with Ken Russell directing. It was a huge set with lots of fake computers about – rather boring things to photograph. But eventually Michael Caine came up a ladder with me to the lighting gantry over the set.

Michael Caine, Pinewood, 1967.

On the back seat of a late 1920s Rolls-Royce lay the essential accoutrements of an English gentleman.

Rolls-Royce rally, Goodwood, 1967.

18 July 1967: I had lunch at the Ivy restaurant. Philip Oakes was interviewing Margaret Lockwood for the Atticus column in the *Sunday Times*. Lockwood was born in India, the daughter of a clerk on the railways. Her film career started with *Lorna Doone* in 1935 and by the time it ended she had made about thirty films, including, in 1967, *The Wicked Lady* with James Mason as her leading man. She went to Hollywood, but soon came back, as the Americans didn't seem to know what to do with her.

When I had lunch with her at the Ivy she was fifty-one, with a sadly slipping career. She died at the age of seventy-four in 1990, leaving a CBE and a daughter, Julia, whom she called Toots.

Margaret Lockwood, the Ivy restaurant, 1967.

June 1967: I went to photograph the tennis championships at Wimbledon – goodness knows why, as I wasn't a sports photographer. The press had whipped the whole nation into a tizz because one of the finalists was British. I have never had a nationalistic streak in me – I hardly know who's British and who isn't – but this afternoon I suddenly felt an awesome sense of responsibility. I thought, supposing I miss the shot or the only shot worth printing is out of focus? This happened once when I photographed Princess Anne galloping across a field, cape flying, at a Benenden School sports day. Quite unusable – but such a good picture!

I needn't have worried, because our Ann Jones was beaten by Billie Jean King and I got some, though I say it myself, surprisingly good photos. This one, of the vanquished Ann Jones just after the match, wasn't used, though I protested that poignancy of the defeated was perhaps more worth publishing than the victorious pictures of Billie Jean King parading around the court with her hard-won trophy.

Two years later Ann Jones was victorious and won the women's title from Billie Jean King. Britain was not to have another singles female title-holder until Virginia Wade won in 1977 against Betty Stove. And none since.

Ann Jones beaten by Billie Jean King, Wimbledon, 1967.

July 1967: *Love in a Mist* was Marianne Faithfull's album that year and I went to photograph her for the *Sunday Times*. She was wearing a Chinese shawl over a blouse and tights, no skirt and a straw hat. Smoking and with a dazzling smile on her face, she looked as though she had rushed back from Ascot for the interview. In her thirties she became a heroin addict. In her fifties, detoxified, she began to sing again.

Marianne Faithfull at a house in Marylebone Road, London, 1967.

24 August 1967: It would be hard for me to think of a more joyful couple than the conductor and pianist Daniel Barenboim and his wife, the cellist Jacqueline du Pré, as I saw them that day, three months after their wedding in Jerusalem. I photographed them in a basement flat in north London, and I immediately felt the warmth of their happiness.

They had five years of exciting professional success until, in 1972, Jacqueline was diagnosed with multiple sclerosis, a disease which prised her from her musical genius and finally drove husband and wife apart. She died in 1987, aged forty-two.

Jacqueline du Pré and
Daniel Barenboim, London,
1967.

Jacqueline du Pré after
receiving an honorary
degree at Oxford in 1984,
three years before her
death.

30 August 1967: After meeting at Claridge's and doing a few pictures with the Duke of Bedford, I went with the Duchess to Cartier's to try on a few earrings.

Duchess of Bedford at Cartier's, 1967.

November 1967: Every year, in the week before Armistice Day, 11 November, people remember the dead in a garden next to Westminster Abbey called the Field of Remembrance. There they write a note to the men and women lost in wars, attach it to a small wooden cross and then push the cross into the ground or softly hammer it home with a mallet. The field is divided by service and regiment. As the week goes on, the ground fills up with thousands of crosses, like a miniature replica of a war cemetery.

Armistice Day, 1967.

24 January 1968: I wondered if David Frost's irreverent attitude would be a problem when I went to Rediffusion studios at Wembley to photograph a production meeting of *Frost on Friday*, one of his enormously popular television shows in which his regard for the sensibilities of authority was nil. I needn't have worried – I don't think he knew I was there.

Frost *on Friday* production meeting, January 1968.

22 March 1968: To meet the poet Robert Graves. Graves was born in 1895 in Wimbledon and led a sheltered middle-class life until, in 1915, he became an officer in the Royal Welch Fusiliers and was sent to fight in the trenches of northern France. When I met him in 1968, his translation of *The Rubáiyát of Omar Khayyám*, which he wrote with Omar Ali-Shah, was causing great academic interest. Some said that the Graves–Shah translation was much truer to the original than the version by Edward FitzGerald, which was so free as to be almost an original work. The moving finger writes, and having writ moves on, etc.

Robert Graves with his and FitzGerald's versions of The Rubáiyát, London, 1968.

20 April 1968: I drove on this beautiful spring day to Badminton in Gloucestershire, where the Queen, Prince Philip and the Queen Mother were attending the horse trials. I'd been sent to get 'sensational' pictures of them. I was lucky with one. I trained my camera on the royal Land Rover in the hope that, when it stopped, the Queen and Queen Mum would get out for a wander or something. They did and I got this chorus-line picture, best legs forward.

Their Majesties Queen Elizabeth II and Queen Elizabeth the Queen Mother at Badminton, 1968.

Queen Elizabeth, Badminton horse trials, 1968.

11 May 1968: News was coming in that Paris was erupting in student riots. I took a plane and got there by noon. I knew I had to be back in the office by 4 or 5 o'clock – this was a Saturday, when the *Sunday Times* went to press – which meant catching a plane from Le Bourget Airport at 2.30 p.m. I had about ninety minutes to get a picture. I kept my taxi from the airport waiting for me in a side street while I walked around the Left Bank. Nothing much was happening. Then suddenly, in the Boulevard St Michel, the police started lobbing tear gas at the students. By 1.30 I thought I had a reasonable picture, so I found my taxi and we drove to the airport, arriving there five minutes before take-off. I pleaded with the desk to hold the plane – 'I have to get the film back on this plane or it will be too late' – and they did. It's not a fantastic picture but I was told that it was the only one of the Paris riots that morning.

The process, as well as the event, now seems historic. The days have long gone when pictures needed a photographer to take them home.

Paris, May 1968.

20 May 1968: At the hospital in Henley-on-Thames my wife, Lisa, was lying on the bed screaming as she tried to ease the pain of her first child. I tried holding her hand but it didn't help. I took some photographs. Then we were told she must go to Reading hospital, where they had better facilities to cope with the baby being in a bad position. The ambulance came and we dashed off to Reading. There our daughter Sam was born and we were all very happy.

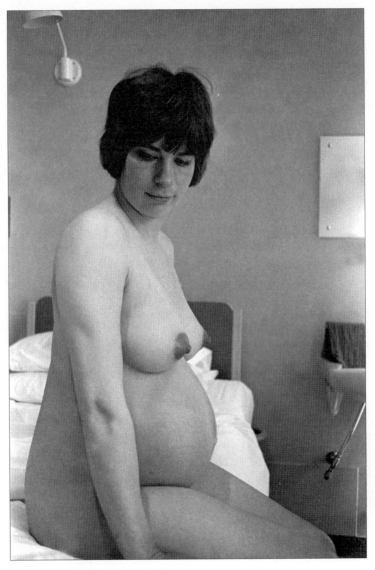

Lisa just before the pain started.

The pain.

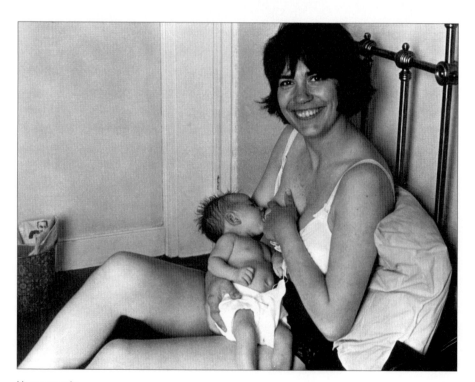

Home again.

194

3 July 1968: Wonderful to be able to photograph Alicia Markova, but what do you do with one of the world's finest ballet dancers when the venue for the shots is a London hotel? I took her into the gardens opposite the hotel and parked her on a bench. Not much chance of capturing her grace and flow of movement in that position either, I thought, until I was suddenly aware that she was dancing sitting down.

Alicia Markova, London, 1968.

10 October 1968: 'Little old lady passing by' — after she passed, she came back to apologize for spoiling my picture. I said I couldn't have done it without her.

John Updike, American novelist, was being interviewed by Alan Brien in the unlikely location of Highgate Cemetery, north London. Updike's novel *Couples* had just been published.

John Updike talking to Alan Brien, 1968.

1969: It should have been a happy year. Although Granny Willoughby died, Lisa was pregnant again. We had a comfortable life in the Old Farm House at Russell's Water near Henley. I had a marvellous job at the *Sunday Times*. Friends and family came to visit. We bought our beer by the barrel. We had two cars – a green drop-head Rolls Bentley and a red Mini estate – and a black and beautiful Blüthner grand. I thought, what more could we want? The answer must have been something, because the monumentals still carried on.

Sam and the beautiful black Blüthner, 1969.

22 January 1969: With Philip Oakes to the National Portrait Gallery to photograph Dr Roy Strong, recently elevated from Assistant Keeper to Director – thirty-three years old and charming, though odd.

Oddball: Dr Roy Strong, Director, National Portrait Gallery, 1969.

May 1969: This was the Rolls-Royce answer to the government's decree that the mascot of a motor car, even the one that graced a Rolls-Royce, the *Spirit of Ecstasy* by Charles Sykes, should collapse on impact with a person with whom it is in head-on collision.

The Spirit of Ecstasy by Charles Sykes bending to the spirit of the moment, May 1969.

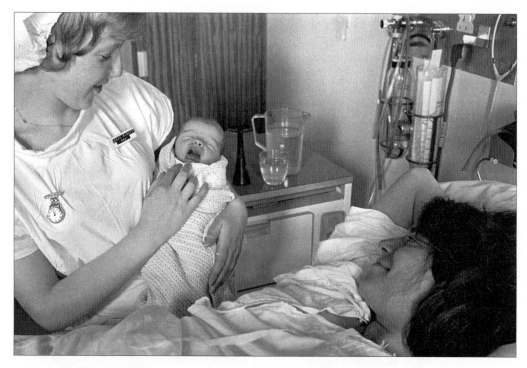

Our second daughter, Tasha, was born at the Royal Berkshire Hospital on 27 June 1969.

Claire Bloom on set at Pinewood, 1969.

1 July 1969: To Hampstead to photograph Peter Cook for an article on the 'Look' pages of the *Sunday Times* called 'Me and My Money' (which preceded a series called 'Me and My Bra'). Because I laughed myself near to death when I saw Peter Cook on screen, especially when he was with Dudley Moore, I was shocked to find that with me he was merely polite and pleasant.

Peter Cook, Hampstead, 1969.

Christopher Logue, Notting Hill, 1969.

Christopher Logue had just published a book of poems called *New Numbers* and I went to photograph him in Notting Hill in July 1969. He seemed a tough character – he made me slightly nervous. He'd served with the Black Watch in Egypt and spent over a year in an army jail for having too many pay-books in his possession. He did other things apart from poetry – a column for *Private Eye* and acting in a couple of Ken Russell films and a screenplay for a third. His reputation was firmly established with his translations of Homer's *Iliad*, published between 1988 and 1994.

One morning in early January 1969 the picture desk rang to ask if I would go with Philip Oakes to photograph Elizabeth Seal, who had just started rehearsals for a Feydeau farce called *Cat Among the Pigeons* at the Prince of Wales, Leicester Square. I hadn't seen or spoken to her for nine years. She'd been living in America, where she'd married for a second time. Her new husband was Zack Matalon, an actor from the Broadway run of *Irma*, and they had three children together: Adam, Sarah and Noah. The marriage was now disintegrating, but I didn't know this when I went with Philip to her flat in Earls Court and took her pictures. My diary merely says, 'Pix of Elizabeth Seal – delicious lady'.

Then in July she rang to ask if I would do some private pictures. I did, and when I took the contacts to her dressing room after the show one night, I asked her to dinner at a restaurant ridiculously called the Romantica. I pathetically excused my behaviour by telling myself that the job would make a little extra money. From then on, late at night, I took the dogs for a walk past the village telephone box. I had to talk to her. The rows with Lisa, which we had been having since our honeymoon, began to get worse – not because of my affair with Elizabeth, my concealment tactics were too good for that, but because when we were alone we didn't seem able to control our depression or our anger. For a year I met Elizabeth secretly, and then I couldn't cope any more and I had to let Lisa and the children down.

Elizabeth Seal in Earls Court. January 1969.

30 July 1969: I went to photograph Joan Crawford, whose acting I'd always admired. She was filming *Trog* at the Bray studios near Maidenhead, and Philip Oakes was writing a feature on her for the *Sunday Times*.

It was late on a summer evening. Before wrapping up, the camera crew were catching the last rays of the sun, and the last rays of the sun were catching Crawford's face. I loved her lines. She was sixty-three, still beautiful, and I thought her lines gave her a radiant calmness. She didn't share this view of herself, however, and wrote this letter to Philip Oakes. Alas, I was told that the picture was also used in the *New York Times* the next week.

G H

GROSVENOR HOUSE
P.O.BOX No. 961
PARK LANE
LONDON W 1 Y 4E D

Telephone : 01-499 6363
Telegrams : Grovhows London W.1
Telex : 24871

9th August 1969

Philip Oakes, Esq.
The Sunday Times
Thomson House
200 Gray's Inn Road
London W.C.1

Philip dear,

Thank you so much for your letter of August 5th. I am so deeply grateful to you for explaining the reason for the horrendous picture that was printed.

Had I been Michael Ward, I never would have presented the lousy pictures to "The Times" or anybody. I would have just said that these are the best I could get and not give the editor the bad ones, only the good ones, whether I lost the job or not. After all, his name is on the picture, not mine, thank God.

Bless you, your letter meant a great deal to me.

Love Joan

Joan Crawford at Bray studios, July 1969.

28 August 1969: I was sent to Manchester to photograph racial tension. Riots were reported to be imminent. There were none. All I could find were indications of racial harmony. Tension, unless it manifests itself in violence, is an impossible thing to demonstrate visually.

Racial tension, Manchester, 1969.

10 September 1969: To somewhere in Chelsea to photograph the American actress Lee Remick, who had probably just finished filming *Loot* – Joe Orton's black comedy which was such a success in the theatre.

She had penetrating eyes which challenged you to say something interesting – a stimulating performance. She was easier than most actresses to talk with because she managed to talk about things other than herself, and she also came out with phrases such as 'Breasts and bottoms are boringly alike.' She died much too young in 1991, at the age of fifty-five.

Lee Remick, London, 1969.

The novelist Kingsley Amis at his home near Barnet, 1969.

By the time the 1960s ended, the *Sunday Times* had established itself as 'one of the world's great newspapers' — the slogan decorated the sides of the vans that delivered the papers from the presses in the Gray's Inn Road to newsagents, wholesalers and trains for the north at the London termini. The presses were in the basement. Above them were floors for advertising and accounts, then the composing room and eventually, on floors four, five and six, the editorial departments. On the fifth floor, photographers worked out of a corner of the newsroom where the picture desk was located. Next to it were the desks for reporters, every one with a black telephone and a sit-up-and-beg typewriter, with a long desk for the sub-editors just across the passageway. Several of the sub-editors smoked pipes and each was equipped with the tools of his trade: scissors for cutting copy, a pot of glue to paste copy together, a spike for redundant copy, a pencil to edit copy. Messengers (men again) would answer the call of 'Copy!' and stuff it into canisters, which were taken by a sucking and hissing pneumatic tube to the hot-metal Linotype machines in the composing room. There were very few women: a secretary or two, a couple of reporters, an assistant on the picture desk, and the lady who steered the tea trolley.

The week usually began quietly and sociably. There was almost nobody around on Monday. On Tuesdays and sometimes Wednesdays — days in which the shape of the paper was still being determined — one could sit around a bit and chat and go for a long lunch. Then the jobs came up: a story in Inverness, a conference in Birmingham, a film star at Pinewood, the Miss World contest, a National Front demonstration, a portrait of a company chairman for the Business News section. It was often luck (or bad luck) that decided which photographer got which job, depending on whether you happened to be in the office and free when an assignment came up. Then you would be off to stand about in the rain for four hours, waiting for Elizabeth Taylor, or to Badminton to watch royalty falling from their horses.

Under the editorship first of Denis Hamilton and then of Harold Evans, the *Sunday Times* had become a courageous, innovative and continually interesting newspaper and I knew I was lucky to be there. But it was not always an easy place to be. The picture desk could be a quarrelsome little corner (there were historic divisions) and I suppose I had a carefree way of behaving which wasn't completely justified by my technical abilities. The best hard-news photographer on the paper was Steve Brodie, who always managed to be in the right place at the right time with the right shutter speed and bring back pictures which could comment on a story as well as illustrate it. His pictures had a purposeful directness which reflected his personality. I always found directness very difficult – the more oblique approach was my line and I was quite happy if I felt the picture was good, regardless of whether or not it was directly connected to the story. I was once sent to cover an Arsenal football match at their home ground, just a mile or two from the office in north London. Arsenal had (and has) a rich support. I came back with a picture of Rolls-Royces parked outside the ground; while their owners watched the game, the chauffeurs stood beside their charges, drinking coffee from plastic cups. The picture was liked and published, but my pictures of the game itself were thought to be so poor that agency pictures had to be substituted. I was never sent to do football again.

When Steve Brodie was promoted to picture editor I expected trouble ahead and sure enough it came. He was gruff and tough, and liked to play tricks on the unsuspecting, like an old army sergeant might with new recruits. Once he asked me if I had seen his new skill with karate. With one blow, he could divide a packet of cigarettes in two and leave every cigarette undamaged.

He then placed my full packet of Dunhill on the desk and, with a flourish, smashed it with his fist. There was a hardly a cigarette left that was still smokable. 'Ah, sorry,' he said, 'it hasn't worked.' Another time I was over on the other side of the newsroom, talking to the reporter, when Steve looked up from my contacts and roared, 'Michael – you're a failed pianist, a failed actor, and now you're a bloody awful photographer.'

The newsroom fell silent. Not for the first time, I was mortified.

10 January 1970: My dear beloved grandfather Harold Willoughby was buried today. He was eighty-seven. Because he believed in spiritualism, he had stipulated that there was to be no reference to God in the funeral service. My father used to say that he was a saint – partly, because he was astonishingly patient with Granny, who hardly drew a breath without talking. So now they have both gone.

Grandfather and Granny Willoughby in North Wales, *circa* 1963.

20 February 1970: To Soho with a reporter for a story about teenage prostitutes. I talked to one in a café about the tricks of her trade. She was sixteen. The best thing, she said, was to get the money without delivering the goods. 'There are many ways of getting away with it. Like, having persuaded my client to pay in advance, I say, "Wait here, darling, while I pop into the chemist's. I've got to get some condoms." And I leave the chemist's by the back door.' She worked out of a room in a collapsing eighteenth-century house whose front door opened on to an alley, which opened on to Berwick Street market. The alley was used to dump unsold crates of rotting vegetables. I remembered that twenty-five years earlier, when I occasionally used their services, their conditions were better – and they weren't teenagers.

Teenage prostitute, Soho, London, 1970.

10 March 1970: Eileen Atkins lived in a flat which looked over the roofs of the mews houses at the back of Ennismore Gardens in Kensington. She was a quiet lady with a beautiful face, but also somehow a sad one, so I thought I would bring where she lived into the photograph. In the distance is the Brompton Oratory. The last time I saw Atkins, in 2003, she was giving a lovely portrayal of Philip Larkin's mother in a fine television drama documentary of his life. For her career in the theatre she was made a Dame of the British Empire in 2001.

Eileen Atkins, London, 1970.

12 March 1970: George Dobson had been a miner at the now long-defunct Clare Vale pit in Durham. He was sixty-seven and slowly dying from pneumoconiosis, which he contracted by breathing coal dust during his life underground. He was claiming damages and hoping to receive reasonable compensation, but there was nothing one could do or say that might alter the hopeless acceptance I saw in his face.

Miner George Dobson, pneumoconiosis victim, Durham, 1970.

15 April 1970: For all his camp flamboyance, Frankie Howerd was difficult to photograph — he seemed so self-conscious. Finally, I tried shooting from the ground, and he said, 'I'll squash you like the worm that you are.' I was there because of his performance as a Roman slave called Lurcio in the musical *Up Pompeii*.

Frankie Howerd, Kensington, London, 1970.

21 June 1970: Journalist Philip Oakes and his photographer Michael Ward (a phrase to which I always had a silent objection) went to the Dorchester to see Peggy Lee, who was in town for the first time in nine years. To me Peggy Lee was up there with jazz singers like Billie Holiday, Sarah Vaughan, Ella Fitzgerald and Anita O'Day. She had done a long stint with Benny Goodman, which of course endeared her to me. Her singing made an artist out of a professional. In her Dorchester suite I felt frustrated and slightly disappointed. She didn't look her best; she was a bit overweight and was much too busy talking to Philip. I realized that to get the best picture I needed to be alone with her. There was no time.

I had a 'thank you for sending the photographs' letter from her on a card with a drawing of her face on it, on which she said, 'You really are a pleasant person and I do hope to meet you again one day!' Well, I had three or four Christmas cards from her and we did meet again twice, first when she played the London Palladium and last at Hatchards bookshop, where she was signing copies of her autobiography.

Peggy Lee, Dorchester Hotel, 1970.

October 1970: I'd been having an affair with Elizabeth Seal since July the previous year. We spent as much time together as we could – occasionally she came on jobs with me – and it became clear that my deception of my wife and children, and the guilt that came with it, were impossible to sustain. I knew I wasn't able to give the rest of my life to Lisa; the desolation and the monumentals we had were becoming unbearable. I'm sure it must have been the same for her. I told her about Elizabeth and me. At first she was very composed, but then she was extremely upset and the fights began. Drink was drunk, sleep was forgotten and some very nasty things were said. She said that what was hurting her was not that I was not in love with her and never had been – she said she felt the same way about me – but that I had shattered her dream of having children, a home and a husband, and that I should never have married her. Our talking went on night after night – one moment clear thoughts and understanding, the next moment, confusion and bitterness.

Elizabeth had gone to America to see her children, Adam, Sarah and Noah, who were living with their father, Zack, and his new partner, Suzannah. I wrote, asking her to share my life as soon as possible: 'I think it's so wonderful that I've met you. – To meet someone with whom the two avenues of feeling – tender affection and primitive passion – are united is very rare. You're delicious – let me hear you laugh soon.' Then I flew to New York, where we spent a few days at Elliot Gould's flat (he was with her in *Irma La Douce*) and prepared ourselves for the traumatic meetings with Zack at what had been Elizabeth's marital home in Harrison, Maine.

Zack, Suzannah and the children met our Greyhound bus and whisked us off to see a drive-in movie, a bizarre start to a fortnight of angry discussions which sometimes took place in an atmosphere of fear and violence: Zack told us he had a gun in the top drawer of the bureau in the bedroom and once, when Elizabeth stood scared and rooted by the door, spent a long ten minutes bouncing a tennis ball off her.

Eventually we left with Elizabeth's youngest child, Noah – Zack refused to surrender the passports for Sarah and Adam. It was a terrible decision for Elizabeth to make, between choosing to stay with all her children in the family home, and therefore also with Zack and Suzannah, and taking only Noah and being with me. Back in London, the three of us set up home in Elizabeth's old flat up four flights of stairs in Earls Court Road, together with Django and

Tarquin, my Alsatian and my Labrador. Elizabeth looked for work in the theatre. We had very little money; all I could afford to send Lisa and the children was £100 a month. We looked for a house to mortgage without a deposit.

24 October 1970: Two oil tankers, the *Pacific Glory* and the *Allegro*, had collided just off the Isle of Wight. Reporter Wendy Hughes and I hired a boat which took us to within around 300 yards of the blazing wreck of the *Pacific Glory*, until the heat was so great that we had to back off. This picture reminds me of newspaper pictures we saw during the Battle of the Atlantic in the Second World War.

Pacific Glory ablaze off the Isle of Wight, 1970.

The pit head at Celynen Pit, Western Valley, Newbridge, South Wales. The miners are on strike. At lunch with them in their canteen, they tell me stories of the disaster at Abercarn pit in 1878: 250 souls lost after an explosion – rescue was impossible, so the owners flooded the pit and drowned them. Other stories of small coffins being kept in houses prior to 1926, waiting for the next child to die of starvation.

Celynen Pit, South Wales, 1970.

14 November 1970: The Lord Mayor's Show. This has been going on since 1215. The Lord Mayor is elected every year and the day of his instalment is celebrated by a procession through the streets of the City of London, usually ending up with a feast at Guildhall, where leading statesmen pompously put their point of view.

Lord Mayor's Show, London, 1970.

27 November 1970: A job in the office! I had to take a picture of the editor. Harry (Harold) Evans came to the *Sunday Times* from the *Northern Echo* in Darlington in 1967 and edited the paper between 1967 and 1981, when the new proprietor, Rupert Murdoch, made him editor of *The Times*. He resigned a year later in response to the pressure Murdoch was putting on his editorial independence. At the *Sunday Times*, his enterprise, energy and egalitarianism won the respect and affection of his staff and made him one of the best-loved editors in Fleet Street's history.

Harry Evans, editor, 1970.

Like a giant ocean liner, Battersea Power Station dominates the surrounding metropolitan chaos which it powered for so many years. After it closed, it was nearly resurrected as a shopping and amusement park but the scheme fell through. For many years it has joined the empty cathedrals across the land, its vast emptiness posing the question, 'Where did we go wrong?'

Battersea Power Station, London, 1970.

31 December 1970: My last picture of a very difficult year. Went with Michael Bateman, who was writing the Atticus column, to see the New York writer and wit S. J. Perelman, who scripted two Marx Brothers films. He was in his mid-seventies and had that easy American charm that is sometimes so disarming – lots of energy, very amusing in a droll sort of way, but inclined to go on a bit. Sense of timing waning – perhaps?

S. J. Perelman, London, 1970.

February 1971: A tug on my heart's memory. I went with Philip Oakes to Baron's Keep, off the Cromwell Road extension, to interview John Le Mesurier, who played twitchy bureaucrats in British films for as long as I could remember and became very famous as a star in *Dad's Army* on BBC television. A great fan and friend of my father, a greater fan of the jazz pianist Art Tatum, and a lovable, softly spoken gentleman. We talked of many things, including that day in 1939 when he and my father dumped me at Lake House School, Bexhill.

John Le Mesurier, London, 1971.

facing page: Noah (left) with Elizabeth and my children, Tasha and Sam, and our dog Tarquin, East Acton, 1971.

7 February 1971, a Sunday: I decided at breakfast this morning that I was a very successful failure and that it was my lack of education and my emotional instability that had made me so. Walked the dogs with Noah, washed the cars, then shoulder of lamb and rhubarb crumble, after which we watched the old film of *Goodbye Mr Chips* with Robert Donat. What a lovely film: so sad, beautifully directed, lovely performances, everybody crying. Ronnie, my father, was in it: he played an old boy looking as I used to know him when I was at school.

Soon after this diary entry we moved to a house we'd bought in Wells House Road, East Acton, one of series of small streets built in the 1880s to house the families of the men who built the enormous complex of railways in west London (we still have the Great Western Railway oil lamp used by the previous owner's grandfather). The street was predominantly working class. I suppose we were early 'gentrifiers' at a time when London house prices were beginning to take off and houses began to be seen as assets rather than homes. We bought the house for £5,000 and about two years later sold it for £13,500. We bought another for £16,000 in Hampton Wick, Kingston upon Thames, and moved in on 4 December 1973.

28 August 1971: 'Lesbians Come Out' was one of the pleas on the banners of the Gay Liberation March which camped in Trafalgar Square. Everybody was having a good time, even the gentleman who had come to look at the lions.

Gay Lib March, Trafalgar Square, London, 1971.

Penelope Mortimer, London, 1971.

7 September 1971: Penelope Mortimer created a formidable and slightly intimidating front of sexual intelligence when Philip Oakes and I went to see her,
though Oakes appeared to have the immediate future under control.

Her best-known novel, *The Pumpkin Eater*, became a highly successful film
with Anne Bancroft, Peter Finch and James Mason, directed by Jack Clayton.
Later she wrote a controversial biography of the Queen Mother. She was married for more than twenty years to the barrister, playwright and novelist John
Mortimer and died in 1999.

2 December 1971: The press were invited to RAF Fairford to experience the new supersonic aircraft, Concorde, built jointly by Britain and France, on a flight to Lisbon and back. Once aboard, we were in a rather cramped tube with no awareness of the visual delight that was so striking on the tarmac. When the lights came up and expressed proudly that we had passed the speed of sound, there was no indication that we were travelling at more than the London speed limit. Slightly disappointing. Even more disappointing was the fact that we never got to Lisbon at all. While drinking large amounts of champagne, I noticed a little red light winking and casually asked the flight engineer sitting by me what it was. He thanked me and said that the port engine was over-heating. Well – of course – we immediately left the Bay of Biscay and cruised slowly back to Fairford.

Concorde, RAF Fairford, 1971.

My diary entry for 15 January 1972:

> Forty-three today – hair nearly white – too fat – bronchitis – can't give up
> smoking – no money – too many commitments – otherwise I had a very
> happy birthday.

The next month I had a marvellous Business News job when I flew to Paris
with reporter Philip Clarke and a PR for Martell's cognac, and then took a train
to Angoulême, where a car picked us up and drove us to Martell's guest
house – the Château de Chanteloup. There we were alone with a butler and a
bottle of Martell Cordon Bleu. Next day at breakfast there were bacon and eggs
and a choice of brandy. A tour of distilleries and vineyards then commenced.
In an old shed known as Maison du Paradis I was given a blend of 1848 and 1875
cognacs – like nothing I've drunk before or since – and managed to shoot a few
pictures. Michel Martell then showed us his house, where he was immensely
proud of a monstrous coffee table made of rhino skin and elephant tusks, both
taken from animals he had shot. We had Cordon Bleu after every meal for
three days, and it was an effort to resist taking the casual bathroom bottle
home with me.

After the job (if it could be so defined) was finished, I hired a car in
Bordeaux and drove to Rouffignac and on to Lajarthe, where Lisa was living
with our children, Sam and Tasha, and a young man, François Retif, whom she
had met in France the year before. Sam and Tasha were glad to see me and
screamed with delight. Everyone seemed happy. François was very charming
and young, and Sam and Tasha seemed to like him. Lisa said, 'He's so unsuit-
able!' but she also told me that she had found her sexual self-respect. (Some
time later they had a daughter, Alice Retif.) On my last day there Sam, Tasha
and I had a picnic in one of the caves near Les Eyzies, where, 40,000 years ago,
Neanderthal man was doing much the same thing. We had a wonderfully
happy time, but by the evening I was very miserable: they were going to
Switzerland with Lisa and François to see Natalia, Lisa's mother, and I didn't
know when I would be seeing them again. Sam and Tasha were in their py-
jamas for the night drive to Switzerland. There were lots of hugs and kisses. I
drove behind them for about three miles, as far as Le Moustier, all the while
seeing Sam's little face watching me through the back window of Lisa's car. We

stopped together at a garage. More hugs and kisses and strained laughter, then they drove off. I cried so much I had to stop the car and go for a walk.

27 June 1972: A hot summer's day. I was photographing in a garden in a village called Leigh, in Surrey, with Mia Farrow and her two young sons, Sascha and Matthew. We did a few pictures around the lawn and then went to the kitchen for coffee. She was much happier talking than posing, but I wished her then husband, André Previn, had been there too; he was one of my favourite jazz pianists. Farrow, whose first brief marriage was to Frank Sinatra, had six children (three adopted) with Previn and went on to have three more (two adopted) with Woody Allen. By the time she was forty-nine she had a total of fourteen children, five of them her own.

Such eyes!

Mia Farrow, Surrey, 1972.

Gypsy Moth V returns, 1972.

Linked together on a plaque in Westminster Abbey are Sir Francis Drake, Captain James Cook and Sir Francis Chichester. At the end of June 1972, despite being diagnosed with cancer at the base of his spine, Chichester entered the fourth single-handed race across the Atlantic on his yacht *Gypsy Moth V*. Unhappily, his illness overcame him and he had to turn back. On 1 July we spotted him from a chartered plane after three or four hours scouring the Western Approaches, his yacht surging through the waves and looking as brave as he was having to be.

233

9 August 1972: To Liverpool with Anne Robinson, the most glamorous reporter on the paper, on another story about racial unrest. On the street a couple came towards me, one white, one black, hand in hand. I said, 'I'm from the *Sunday Times*. Would you mind telling me how long you've been as happy as you look?' They looked at me a trifle nonplussed, so I added, 'I've been – that is, me and the *Sunday Times* have been told that there is a lot of racial unrest in this area of Liverpool.' The answer was, 'Look', and the woman stroked her black companion's cheek. 'It doesn't come off – even after years of marriage!'

Racial tension, Liverpool, 1972.

234

12 August 1972: To yet another pop festival, this time in Reading. It was the same old thing – hot, dusty and for me, a jazz fan, the sound of terrible music. Then I saw Sadie, Mame and Millie. They called themselves Three Tons of Joy. They were a singing act and they were really huge and happy.

Sadie, One Ton of Joy, Reading, 1972.

22 November 1972: With Philip Oakes again to interview the playwright John Osborne. I expected to find him irascible, rude and unhelpful. He was charm itself. When I asked him to move a standard light out of the way, he not only obliged but held it for me so I could get this shot.

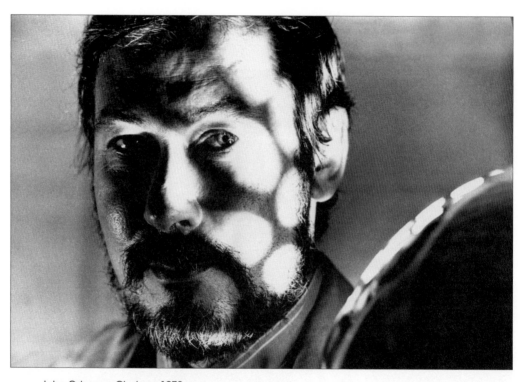

John Osborne, Chelsea, 1972.

7 December 1972: Stopped by the police for speeding on the M4 on my way to photograph the composer Michael Tippett; I was late. One of his recordings had been voted the record of the year. He lived with his partner in a house overlooking a beautiful expanse of Wiltshire and there was an immediate easy communication between us. He was, however, a little perplexed when I wanted to go outside to photograph him inside.

Sir Michael Tippett, Wiltshire, 1972.

Early in 1973 I went to Sussex University to photograph Professor Quentin Bell – a lovely, friendly man. He told me he was Virginia Woolf's nephew. I didn't know that – once again I noticed how uneducated I was. I suppose our assistant picture editor assumed I knew, or perhaps he didn't know himself. Bell had been awarded the Duff Cooper Prize for his biography of his aunt and I enjoyed talking to him enormously – about writing and about the sexual proclivities of the Bloomsbury Group. In fact I was so taken with him and his subject that I spent six non-reclaimable pounds on his two-volume biography.

Professor Quentin Bell, Sussex University, 1973.

March 1973: I borrowed £500 from the *Sunday Times* to be paid back in three months and cashed some Premium Bonds and a Post Office Savings Account to make up £600 to buy a six-foot eleven-inch model-B Steinway grand piano. It was rosewood and, although aged a little since 1905, it was elegantly wonderful and shone in our fourteen foot square front room.

I went to a quiet Georgian square at the back of Oxford Street to take pictures of Peter Maxwell Davies for the Gulbenkian Foundation. He was blue-chinned with wild, wiry hair, thin lips and startling eyes. He looked like Beethoven.

Peter Maxwell Davies, London, 1973.

April 1973: A £1 10p taxi ride with Philip Oakes to Hampstead to interview and photograph Alan Ayckbourn, prolific writer of theatre comedies about the woes and hopes of the middle classes. He lived in a flat with a tiny yard of a garden and was amusing and affable, and he made me feel as though I was in one of his plays. He had just finished producing his trilogy *The Norman Conquests*.

Alan Ayckbourn, London, 1973.

29 July 1973: To Sweden with Oliver Gillie, the *Sunday Times*'s medical correspondent, for a story about the development of the medieval birthstool to a twentieth-century stainless steel birth chair in which a mother is nearly standing. We watched as a sixteen-year-old unmarried mother had her baby sitting up in a birth chair designed by Dr Christman Ehrstrom, who had noticed that one of his patients who was thought to need a Caesarean operation gave birth naturally after sitting upright for about ten minutes. He has now delivered more than sixty babies with their mothers sitting in his chair. The picture was controversial in the office and Harry Evans showed it to his secretary, Joan Thomas (ex-Darlington, ex-Salvation Army), who passed it fit for publication.

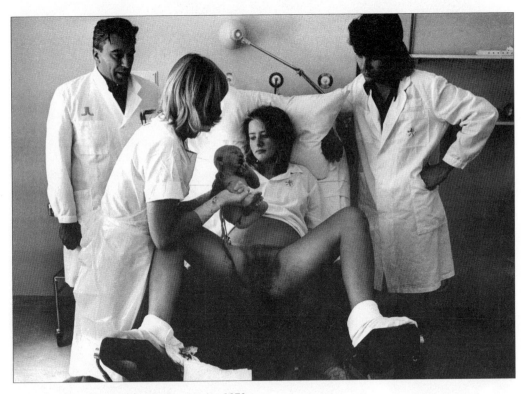

Swedish birth chair birth, Stockholm, 1973.

August 1973: To the Globe Playhouse in Southwark to photograph Vanessa Redgrave playing Cleopatra in *Antony and Cleopatra*. Redgrave has a face that makes you look to see what is going to happen next. One looks to see if it is really as beautiful as it appears to be; then suddenly it falls into a pose that is sheer perfection.

Vanessa Redgrave as Cleopatra, London, 1973.

The Great Gatsby: Farrow, Clayton and Robert Redford, 1973.

October 1973: I got a nice picture of Sir John Betjeman at Christ Church College, Oxford, where he was attending the memorial service for W. H. Auden. Betjeman became the Poet Laureate in 1972 and died in 1984.

John Betjeman, Oxford, 1973.

13 February 1974: Sister Pat's birthday today – she would have been forty-seven. I often wonder if she would have helped me to be more emotionally stable. I really enjoyed the last few days with Elizabeth in Leicester [she was playing Sally Bowles in *Cabaret*] but I also felt very depressed and frustrated. I want to create. Photography isn't enough – if only I had been proficient with my piano playing. Maybe I just need to be needed, admired, any kind of superficial attention, a throw-back to the shallow conceit of my adolescent days – my indolescent days! Another talk with Elizabeth about my upbringing – she called it a cruel disgrace. Yet I found it hard to blame anybody but myself.

14 February 1974: To photograph Osbert Lancaster at the *Daily Express* in Fleet Street, where he has been resident pocket cartoonist since 1939. He satirized the English upper classes with his masterly creation of characters, famously Maudie Littlehampton.

Osbert Lancaster at his desk in the *Daily Express* office, 1974.

14 May 1974: A year after I took this photograph, Margaret Thatcher defeated Edward Heath to become the first woman to lead the Conservative (or any other major British) Party. When we met at her house in Flood Street, Chelsea, she had obviously prepared herself to be photographed. For a minute, I thought I'd been sent to photograph a rather glamorous pre-Second World War film star. She was then forty-eight.

Margaret Thatcher, Chelsea, 1974.

21 August 1974: I was sent to cover the war in Cyprus which followed the Turkish invasion – a complicated journey, as no planes were being allowed to land in Cyprus, so I went via Tel Aviv and a small charter plane full of journalists from there. In Cyprus I joined up with the paper's reporter, Will Ellsworth-Jones, and we drove to a village called Ayios Seryios, where there had been shooting a few days before. The village was hot and very quiet. Cars had been abandoned with their doors open and through the windows of houses I could see unfinished meals left on tables. The young had fled and the old had been left to their fate. I'd had heard that the village carpenter had been shot three days before, and now round a corner I found him lying on his side in the white dust, his clothes tight on his inflated body. I remember thinking that the blood flowing down the hill looked like the Ganges delta in my school geography book. As I took pictures I felt frightened and exposed.

The carpenter of Ayios Seryios, Cyprus, 1974,

20 February 1975: To the Berlei Bra fitting school with Lorana Sullivan, who's writing a story for Business News. Not exactly embarrassing, but certainly there was some social difficulty. I managed one good photograph, but of course another was used.

Berlei Bra fitting school, London, 1975.

21 June 1975: I photographed Princess Anne opening a fête at Great Somerford in Wiltshire. Even in 1975, palace officials were getting nervous about photographers getting closer than twenty-five to fifty feet, so I was lucky when Princess Anne stopped to look at a stall that had an opening at the back. I was about six feet from her and nervous.

Princess Anne, Great Somerford, Wiltshire, 1975

14 October 1975: A marvellous sunny day with Norman Wisdom. He was fascinated by my bike and insisted on wearing my helmet. He jumped on the bike and stuck his tongue out at me. He just never stopped fooling around – it was as though, if he stopped fooling, the world would stop turning.

Norman Wisdom, London, 1975.

For me, the biggest event of 1976 occurred on 18 December, when I got married for the fifth time. Sally Soames came down to Richmond to photograph the occasion for the *Sunday Times*, and — because the bride was Elizabeth — photographers from other papers also turned up, disbelieving that I could be the groom. Afterwards we went and had eggs on toast in a café near the Theatre Royal, Drury Lane, where Elizabeth was rehearsing for her part in *A Chorus Line*. I went back to the office with champagne, which was passed around in plastic cups. Next day we were astonished to see ourselves on the front of the *Sunday Times* — there couldn't have been much else going on. I look like the father giving the bride away.

DECEMBER 19 1976   No 8010   Price 18p

THE SUNDAY TIMES

High-kick of joy by actress Elizabeth Seal after her marriage at Richmond yesterday to a Sunday Times photographer, Michael Ward. Then on to an 11 am rehearsal for her big part in A Chorus Line with the British company that takes over at Drury Lane next month

The next year, 1977, got off to a terrible start. On 12 January I went to Cardiff to photograph *The Barber of Seville*. After the job I checked in to the office and was asked to ring Elizabeth's agent, Peter Eade. He told me that Michael Bennet, the director of *A Chorus Line*, was going to sack Elizabeth from her part of Cassie at five that afternoon. *A Chorus Line* was a huge Broadway hit and Cassie was a very large part; the London production would have re-established Elizabeth as a West End star. There were only ten more days of rehearsal to go before the first night. How had it happened?

Bennet had just married Donna McKechnie, who had played Cassie for him on Broadway. When he returned from honeymoon he called a run-through, at which Elizabeth gave only a technical performance because Bennet had told her he was possibly going to rechoreograph her dance. Bennet had not given her any personal direction at all. She had been waiting for this — but it never came. He didn't indicate that anything was wrong, so she wasn't able to work on anything. Halfway through the run-through he told Elizabeth to perform the dance that Cassie does for eight minutes alone. Donna McKechnie, in a sable coat, sat on the stage and watched Elizabeth's performance. By now, Elizabeth had been doing class with the Royal Ballet almost every day for ten months and, after several auditions, had rehearsed the part for more than a month.

At five that afternoon she was shown to a dressing room, where Bennet, Michael White, the producer, and some other men connected with the show's production were waiting for her. Bennet said, 'I'm going to let you go.'

Not quite understanding what he meant, Elizabeth said, 'Excuse me?'

Bennet said, 'Well — I'm going to let you go. I've made a mistake in the casting. There just isn't the right chemistry between you and Jean-Pierre [Cassell, her co-star]. The nature of the play is changing, and anyway I want Donna to play the role.'

Elizabeth said, 'Well, what are you going to tell the press?'

'We could tell them you have injured your ankle or had a nervous breakdown.'

'I don't have nervous breakdowns,' Elizabeth said.

'Then I shall tell them you are too old,' Bennet said.

She was forty-two. Trying to fight back her tears, she said, 'You knew how old I was. It would've been better if you hadn't given me the job at all.'

Her sacking became a story and ran for a couple of weeks in the newspapers. There were demonstrations outside the Drury Lane Theatre, an editorial in the *Evening Standard* and an interview on *News at Ten*.

Elizabeth was touched by so much sympathy, but the wounds inflicted were both professional and personal and she found that the scars they left were difficult to erase.

Elizabeth Seal with a sculpture by John W. Mills of herself as Irma in *Irma La Douce*. I took this picture at the Alwyn Gallery, Grafton Street, Mayfair, on the opening night of *A Chorus Line*, 1977.

Omar Sharif at the *Sunday Times* Bridge Championships, Churchill Hotel, London, January 1977.

26 March 1977: Covered the Stechford, Birmingham by-election today with David Blundy, one of the most talented *Sunday Times* reporters (and certainly the most amusing), who was killed by a bullet in El Salvador in 1989. I still think of his face and manner and miss him.

Shirley Williams, then Labour Minister for Education, now Baroness Williams of Crosby, leader of the Liberal Democrats in the House of Lords, was rushing about from factory to factory in the West Midlands, pleading her political case through a megaphone. Here she is delivering a speech to an enthusiastic crowd.

Shirley Williams, Stechford by-election, 1977.

My mother, Peggy, now seventy-one, took a week off from working at the jew-ellers Carrington's in Bond Street and came with me in the Morris Minor to the Dordogne, where we went on picnics with my children, Sam and Tasha. There were one or two icy moments, but on the whole everybody was as happy as could have been expected.

My mother, Peggy, aged seventy-one, with Sam and Tasha, Dordogne, 1977.

June 1977: Not for the first time, I was sent to cover Trooping the Colour. The picture desk took a fancy to this picture of a part of the crowd in the VIP stand and put it on the front page. The next day I went down to a gala night at Chichester Festival Theatre, where Elizabeth was playing in a review. At dinner after the show we had at our table a slightly inebriated Reginald Bosanquet, the television newsreader whose cheerfully slurred delivery had made him a national celebrity. He broke a lull in the conversation by saying, 'What the hell is Harry Evans doing putting a headless man on the front of the *Sunday Times*? Are we supposed to guess who it is or what? Ridiculous – I say it's Harold Macmillan.' I meekly said that I had taken it. Bosanquet looked at me and said, 'You, sir, are a cunt!' Nevertheless, I saw his point – the picture was what you might call camera-clubby.

Trooping the Colour, Horse Guards Parade, London, 1977.

11 August 1977: The Queen's visit to Belfast. I flew on an early-morning flight and eventually went to Castle Street, where a confrontation with a Republican march was expected. The marchers arrived, jeering and waving placards, one of them informing us that Her Majesty was the Queen of Death. A bomb went off about 200 yards away, injuring some people. A sports car was turned over and set alight. Bricks, bottles and golf clubs came flying over the army barricades and I kept my camera up to my eyes, as much to protect myself as to take pictures. I was tired, frightened and making a tremendous effort to keep calm.

Out of this mayhem came two middle-aged women, who appeared totally unruffled. They walked towards me, through the missiles and past a crouching line of soldiers, chatting as though nothing unusual was occurring.

Conversation during the Queen's visit to Belfast, 1977.

13 August 1977: To Lewisham, south London, for a National Front march, which was attacked by a counter-demonstration of the Socialist Workers Party. The police were defending the National Front's right to march by coming down hard on the opposition. At the invitation of the police, I parked my motorbike outside Lewisham police station – wisely, I thought, until I noticed a plume of smoke rising from its direction. My bike had been set alight by an angry crowd from the SWP. 'Oh, sorry,' they said. 'We thought it was a police bike.' Insurance and the *Sunday Times* paid for a new one.

My motorcycle burning at Lewisham, 1977.

259

2 November 1977: To Manchester and back by bike to photograph Ken Dodd, the great comedian from Liverpool, who once told 1,500 jokes non-stop in three and a half hours, so breaking the previous record for this unnecessary achievement and winning a place in *The Guinness Book of Records*. I photographed him (with his Tickling Stick) because he was starting a campaign to save the Palace Theatre, a splendid Victorian variety house with an interior from 1891. This was the theatre where Elizabeth had her first opening night, in the chorus in *Gay's the Word*, Ivor Novello's last show, in 1950.

Ken Dodd, Palace Theatre, Manchester, 1977.

In January 1978 I went to New York to photograph Benny Goodman, who in my book was probably the greatest clarinet player the world has ever known. It was a speculative venture on my part – I hoped to persuade the *Sunday Times Magazine* to do a story. Perhaps my real motive was simply a wish to spend time in his company – I was a big fan of a man who, aged thirteen, had played alongside Bix Beiderbecke and had formed his own band by 1934. I'd been listening to him since I was a schoolboy in the 1940s. Singers of the calibre of Peggy Lee, Billie Holiday, Ella Fitzgerald and, once, Frank Sinatra sang and recorded with him, but perhaps the most memorable moment of his band's career came in 1938, when they played the first jazz concert ever at Carnegie Hall with a line-up that included Count Basie piano, Teddy Wilson piano, Harry James trumpet, Gene Krupa drums, Lionel Hampton vibraphone and Lester Young tenor sax. The fortieth anniversary of this concert was my excuse to be in New York.

We met at rehearsals at his hotel, and then had lunch, and then again on the day of the concert itself. But I still didn't think I had enough pictures, so I went a day or two later to his apartment on East 66th Street. The doorman said he'd left ten minutes ago, maybe for lunch. I remembered Goodman's favourite restaurant, Oscar's, on 3rd Avenue. 'He's just left,' Oscar said. 'Try Bloomingdale's – he said something about caviar.' It was minus ten degrees, there was snow deep on the streets and I was coming down with flu. None the less, to Bloomingdale's and the caviar counter. No Goodman. I tried the cheese counter. 'Hi there, Mike, what the hell are you doing here? Have some cheese,' said a voice that was unmistakably his. He generously agreed to more pictures and together we went back to his apartment, sliding in the snow with our carrier bags of cheese. I managed to repair his tape recorder and we sat listening to him playing the Mozart clarinet concerto. Although a few thought that when Goodman played and recorded the classics it only came about because of his fame, he was in fact a very fine classical player and had music written for him by Bartók, Morton Gould, Nielsen, Leonard Bernstein, Stravinsky, Aaron Copland and Hindemith. He also recorded Mozart, Beethoven, Brahms and Weber.

He made some coffee. I asked him why he hadn't recorded the Hindemith concerto he had commissioned. He said, 'Well, you know, I was never asked, and I wasn't about to say please.'

My enthusiasm for Goodman never transferred to the colour magazine, which declined to be interested in my pictures. In February they commissioned me for the first and last time to photograph Simon Rattle conducting at the Royal Festival Hall. The results were very underexposed. Poor light and my lack of technical knowledge to blame. Benny Goodman died in 1986.

Benny Goodman keeping fit during rehearsals at Carnegie Hall, 1978.

Benny Goodman in concert, Carnegie Hall, 1978.

6 February 1978: I went to see my father, Ronnie, at his flat in Hampstead, where he grows increasingly melancholy and bad-tempered. He was being given an enema, so I waited outside his room on the landing with Betty and an actor friend of hers. Then Ronnie came out of his room and Betty introduced him to her friend. Ronnie said, 'Bugger off.' Betty tells me that the committee of Denville Hall, the actors' home, have turned Ronnie down for a place there.

25 March 1978: A phone call from Betty. 'Ronnie has been on the floor for one and a half hours and there's nothing I can do about it.'

26 March 1978: Ronnie went into hospital. When I went to see him, he was looking very fragile. He told me that Betty had tried to get him to get up and then had banged his head on the floor several times and hit him on the chest. I asked him if she had banged his head by accident. He said she had done it out of temper. She probably did lose control; she was strained to the limit. He gets things very confused at times. Misinterprets and misunderstands things – but he doesn't lie. There must be some truth in it.

31 March 1978: A summoning phone call from the hospital. I went to his curtained-off bed and found Betty there. Ronnie – a terrible luminous yellow colour – half sitting, leaning to his right as though sleeping. Betty said he died very quietly in his sleep – just slowly stopped breathing. I stroked his still slightly warm head. Betty kissed his cheek. I've always regretted not taking a picture but I didn't, for fear of upsetting Betty.

6 April 1978: My father's funeral at Hendon Park Crematorium. Sadly, no music to break up the usual gibberish about celebrating a life. After the ceremony we wandered about among the memorials, chatting about Ronnie to people we hardly knew. Then two gentlemen from the funeral parlour came up to me and bowed, paused, then said, 'Would you like us to scatter your father or will you take him with you?'

We went back to the house with Betty. Bernard Lee, an actor friend of my father (he was Sergeant Paine in *The Third Man* and 'M' in the first Bond films), played the piano and there was a lot of reminiscing and drink-induced laughter.

10 April 1978: Bryan Wharton, a colleague on the *Sunday Times*, rang this morning to tell me that Steve Brodie, our picture editor, had died of a heart attack. He was forty-five. He could be a difficult man but he was one of the best news photographers in Fleet Street. We'll miss him.

8 June 1978: Harry Evans gave a lunch for the Photographers' Gallery at the Garrick Club, to which he asked members of the photographic trade and Denis Healey, then Chancellor of the Exchequer and a good amateur photographer. Healey made a joke, probably something to do with the bank rate and the fortunes of those present. There was a roar of laughter. I pointed the camera at the sound and clicked the shutter. The flash went off and when I processed the film back at the office I found this picture, which Harry put on the front of the Business News section. A picture of pure luck.

Denis Healey and Harry Evans (fifth and sixth from the left) at a lunch in the Garrick Club, 1978.

By the autumn of 1978 the management and print unions at *The Times* and *Sunday Times* were at war. The management threatened to suspend publication of the titles unless the unions agreed to new working practices. The unions retaliated with unofficial industrial action, which shortened the print run and lost hundreds of thousands of copies. Rumours of closure began to spread around the office. On 30 November the management carried out its threat and suspended publication, though as the journalists were not in dispute we continued to be paid. On the night of the suspension, we had a big party at Langan's Brasserie in Mayfair, attended by stars of stage and screen (including, I think, Jack Nicholson). It was a peculiar event, half-wake, half-affirmation that the paper would return. Some people were bitter about its inappropriateness, but I and many others had a good time till two in the morning.

The papers remained closed through most of 1979 and during the shutdown I did quite a bit of freelance work. In May, when Mrs Thatcher became Prime Minister, my mother exclaimed, 'That dreadful bitch'.

13 July 1979: A very hot day. I rode on the bike to Cuddington, a small village in Buckinghamshire, to photograph John Gielgud, who was on location for a television film. I found him sitting on a gravestone in the graveyard of St Nicholas's Church and eating his lunch. I asked him if he minded if I took some pictures.

'By all means,' he said.

'Do you remember working with my father?' I said.

'And who was your father?' he asked.

'Ronald Ward,' I said.

'Yes, of course, very well indeed. A very good actor.' He paused, then said, 'In a way.' He went on, 'He should have done the classics – he was very nervous. I remember once, it may have been during *The Importance of Being Earnest* at the Globe, I had to push him on stage.'

Ronnie was very impatient with Shakespeare, saying that he couldn't understand a word of it, but he probably said it to amuse people. Ronnie went to secondary school for only one term. Then he went from office boy to the stage of the Islington Empire. Gielgud was educated at Westminster School and went on to train as an actor at the Royal Academy of Dramatic Art.

John Gielgud on location at Cuddington, 1979.

Anna Ford, then ITN news reader, 1979.

12 November 1979: The paper is still closed – there have been times in the past year when it looked as though it would never publish again – but now the future looks brighter. We've begun to do stories again in preparation for its relaunch. I went with John Mortimer, barrister, playwright, novelist (and now, for the *Sunday Times*, journalist), to photograph Marilyn Chambers at Raymond's Revue Bar in Soho. Chambers, born in Connecticut in 1952, began her working life as a model and then got a small part in Barbra Streisand's film *The Owl and the Pussycat*. Thereafter, she had a very successful career as the star of porn films.

Marilyn Chambers at Raymond's Revue Bar, 1979.

17 November 1979: The *Sunday Times* publishes again after a year off the streets. My colleague Sally Soames took this picture of me with some early copies in the newsroom.

MW with the first edition after suspension, 17 November 1979 (photograph by Sally Soames).

Laurence Olivier was playing Lord Marchmain in the television adaptation of Evelyn Waugh's *Brideshead Revisited* when John Mortimer and I went to see him on location at Castle Howard in Yorkshire. Olivier talked a little about Ronnie, my father. He didn't know he had died. John wanted to be photographed with Olivier.

John Mortimer and Laurence Olivier, Castle Howard, 1979.

November 1979: Elizabeth came back from New York to be met by reporters and photographers laid on by Larry Parnes, the producer of the new musical *Chicago*, in which she took over the part of Roxy. I went to Harpenden in Hertfordshire to photograph the nation's best-loved comedian, Eric Morecambe. I tried a double exposure against his garage doors, the only dark background I could find, so that the background would be under-exposed. 'Now lean to your left and look at yourself,' I said. He thought I was mad. He died five years later, in May 1984.

Eric Morecambe at his home in Harpenden, 1979.

Beryl Bainbridge, the novelist, made a rule of never answering the telephone. She had a stuffed buffalo in the front hall of her house in Camden, and a friend, Neville Chamberlain. In the 1960s I often had coffee with her and my friend the painter Austin Davies, her first husband. At the time, she appeared to me to be quite normally eccentric. She was warm, charming and totally absorbed in being herself.

Beryl Bainbridge with her friend Neville Chamberlain, December 1979.

15 January 1980: My birthday (fifty-one) and Elizabeth's first night in *Chicago* at the Cambridge Theatre. A wonderful evening. Hundreds of telegrams. Tumultuous applause. Dressing room packed. Champagne party in the theatre bar.

Elizabeth Seal preparing for her part as Roxy in *Chicago*, London, 27 December 1979.

Michael Frayn at the Greenwich Theatre, London, during rehearsals for his new play, *Liberty Hall*, January 1980.

Anne Howells as 'The Merry Widow' at the London Coliseum, January 1980 (quintuplet exposure).

I went to Claridge's to photograph some old friends of Elizabeth from New York, Garson Kanin and Ruth Gordon. They were married in 1942 and for forty-three years they collaborated in their work and lives, Kanin as an author, playwright, director and screenwriter, Gordon as an actress and writer. He wrote for the stage – among other things, *The Diary of Anne Frank* (1955) and *Funny Girl* (1964). She won an Oscar for Best Supporting Actress for her portrayal of Minnie Castavet in *Rosemary's Baby* (1968). They worked together on films – including *Adam's Rib* (1949) and *Pat and Mike* (1952), with Spencer Tracy and Katharine Hepburn. Ruth died in 1985 and Garson in 1999.

Ruth Gordon with husband Garson Kanin, London January, 1980.

7 March 1980: Went with Jilly Cooper to a late-night interview, with Robert Redford in the Berkeley Hotel. It wasn't until the last shot, when I asked him please to look at me, that I got a decent picture.

Robert Redford, London, 1980.

May 1980: At five in the morning I was on a boat tied up in the middle of the River Tamar in Cornwall, opposite a tiny hamlet called St Clement, trying to photograph an ex-Marine, Guy Sanders, who had brought back a gondola from Venice. The clouds blackened and the wind got up, so that just after I took this shot a squall carried him away downstream and it took two hours for him to get back to me.

A gondola far from home, St Clement, Cornwall, 1980.

No matter how many times I was sent along to Horse Guards Parade to get a picture of Trooping the Colour, I never felt that I had done it too often, that every possible picture had been taken. Regimental colours were first paraded on the monarch's birthday in 1805, and more than 1,400 soldiers and 400 musicians from ten regimental bands always take part. The Queen is there, on horseback until 1987, and the crowds who turn out are always interesting. I tried to get pictures which showed the humanity of it rather than its military precision – this one during a march-past rehearsal before the day itself in 1980.

Trooping the Colour rehearsal, the Mall, 1980.

27 July 1980: To the funeral of Peter Sellers at Golders Green crematorium. Often on solemn occasions such as funerals something happens which disturbs the atmosphere of grief and brings a short respite from the mood of mourning. This happened at Golders Green, when day suddenly turned into night and the rain poured down, causing short-circuits on photographic flash equipment so that cameras flashed repeatedly, turning the scene into a flickering black and white movie. Under the arches where people look at the bouquets and their messages, I saw the saddened face of Britt Ekland, Peter Sellers's ex-wife.

Britt Ekland at the funeral of Peter Sellers, Golders Green, July 1980.

November 1980: Ominous rumblings at the *Sunday Times*. The print unions continued to behave as though they owned the paper, though technology was catching up with them. When I took this picture of the Linotype machines in the composing room I had no idea – very few of us had – that in six years' time such a hot-metal scene would be history.

A sleepy corner of the composing room, the *Sunday Times*, 1980.

23 November 1980: To a terrible earthquake at the small town of San Angelo
dei Lombardi in the mountains near Naples. We had to leave the car and walk
the last two miles up the hill. Ruins everywhere – the town's six churches, the
hospital, the prison, bars and restaurants, apartment blocks, all just huge heaps
of rubble. The town had just collapsed. Down at the cemetery the coffins lay
about so that relatives could identify their families. There was no one in charge.
It was very wet and cold, and the air carried the smell of decomposing people.
I was near to tears trying to photograph the survivors, all the time attempting
to justify what I was doing.

Looking for the dead, Sant'Angelo dei Lombardi, Italy, 1980.

From my mother Peggy's diary, 1 January 1981:

> Michael very tired – I am worried that if he does not get more sleep and
> exercise, he may be very ill. He seems depressed too, also very irritable,
> but not with me. He is angelic!

She was nearly seventy-four but continued to work at Carrington's in Bond
Street.

January 1981: With Stephen Pile of the Atticus column to meet Anita Lasker, a
cellist with the English Chamber Orchestra and a survivor of Auschwitz.

Her musicianship had saved her – she had joined the camp orchestra run
by Alma Rosé, whose mother was the sister of Gustav Mahler. It consisted of
a few fiddles, mandolins, guitars, flutes – and a harmonica. Anita's cello pro-
vided the only bass for all these treble instruments. They played at the main
gate, so that their fellow prisoners could march in step as they were led to and
from work, and sometimes at Sunday concerts.

Anita Lasker, Auschwitz survivor, London, 1981.

We talked for four hours. A TV film, *Playing for Time*, was about to be broadcast and Anita was extremely upset about the distortion of her experience. The truth of the experience, she said, needed no embellishment.

A bargain rejected at Harrods' sale, London, January 1981.

24 January 1981: Rupert Murdoch is trying to buy the paper and came to have a look at his possible purchase. I was introduced to him by Peter Roberts, the managing editor.

Harry Evans shows Murdoch round the *Sunday Times* newsroom 23 January 1981. Left to right: Sally Soames (photographer), Harry Evans, Stephen Arras (reporter), Rupert Murdoch, Will Ellsworth Jones (reporter), Judith Jackson (reporter), Tony Mascarenhas (reporter).

John Ogdon, one of the most brilliant pianists Britain has ever produced, was a patient at the Maudsley Hospital, south London, where he was being treated for a nervous breakdown. He was large and gentle, and greeted us with a warm politeness. We talked for a while in the canteen and then I asked him if he would play for me. He said that the only piano was in the gymnasium. There was a rather rowdy game of netball going on and the piano was in the corner by the punchball and a ping-pong table. He sat at the piano and asked what I would like to hear. I said, 'Can you remember the beginning of Chopin's Ballad in G minor?' and he replied, 'I'll try.' He played it beautifully for about twenty minutes, right through. The sound, though incongruous in the gym, was magical. The netball game didn't stop. Ogdon died in 1989, soon after I photographed him playing again at the Wigmore Hall.

John Ogdon playing Chopin at the Maudsley Hospital, London, January 1981.

3 February 1981: The paper sent me to a Neal Street restaurant in Covent Garden, where Alec Guinness was having lunch with a journalist from the *Express*. As sometimes happened, the *Sunday Times* picture desk had not asked Guinness if he was happy to have his photograph taken. He was a little irritated and asked me to wait outside. He came out of the restaurant dressed in his town gear of dark coat, pigskin gloves and bowler, and his manners were faultless. 'Right, where shall we go?' he said quietly. We walked to Covent Garden where he stood around, braving the stares of passers-by, for about fifteen minutes. He had a delightful charm, both accepting and authoritative. He died in August 2000.

Sir Alec Guinness, Covent Garden, February 1981.

13 February 1981: I was with Frank Giles, our deputy editor, in Amman, waiting on the pleasure of King Hussein to interview and photograph him. We'd been there for two days. This morning Frank said that he had heard on his short-wave radio that Rupert Murdoch had completed his dealings with the unions and had bought *The Times* and the *Sunday Times* from Lord Thomson for £12 million – news that brought both relief and apprehension. An era is over.

King Hussein on his palace balcony, Amman, 1981.

19 February 1981: A sudden meeting in the newsroom, where Harry Evans, almost unable to speak because of his emotion, eventually told us that he was leaving the paper to take over the editorship of *The Times*. We were shocked. Everybody present realized that it was a great loss for us. Frank Giles is now our editor.

Harold Evans tells his staff that he is leaving for *The Times,* February 1981.

I went to Primrose Hill to photograph the composer Elisabeth Lutyens, daughter of the architect Sir Edwin Lutyens. There was some confusion over her address. 'You're late,' Lutyens said. She was more than seventy years of age and sat looking at me like a very old flamingo, with huge black-framed glasses. She was suffering from rheumatoid arthritis. After a while we got on well and she was kindly and tender – but she hated being photographed.

Elisabeth Lutyens, London, 1981.

Another job for the Atticus column. Born Dennis Pratt on Christmas Day in 1908, Quentin Crisp tinted his hair lilac, wore eyeshadow and re-created himself as a walking, witty *objet d'art*. We went along to his bedsit in Chelsea, where he had lived for forty years. The room was filthy. We asked him why he didn't have it cleaned. He declared that there was little point. 'It hasn't been cleaned for forty years – how can it get any dirtier?' He demanded admiration and sympathy rather like a cat or a dog might.

Quentin Crisp, Chelsea, April 1981.

June 1981: Stephen Pile and I drove to Brighton to photograph Dame Flora Robson, one of the great names in British film and theatre. She was eighty. Her face, though not (and never) glamorous, had a quiet enchantment.

Flora Robson, Brighton, 1981.

February 1982: At least twenty photographers and as many journalists spent six hours outside Elizabeth Taylor's house in Chelsea. It was her fiftieth birthday. From about 2 p.m. I stood around in the cold, hoping that whatever was going to happen would happen in daylight. We watched, and some of us photographed, endless deliveries of flowers, a new fridge and policemen going in and out of the house. It had been dark and cold for about two hours when, at twenty minutes past eight, Richard Burton arrived from Geneva, we were told, to take Taylor to her birthday party at Legends nightclub in Old Burlington Street.

About half an hour later Taylor and Burton emerged and the police lost all control. Photographers stood on cars as they struggled for a picture and, above the general clamour, the couple could be heard swearing heartily as they tried to get to their car. They seemed pretty drunk. I waited at the front of the car and flashed a shot at the windscreen.

Richard Burton and Elizabeth Taylor on her fiftieth birthday, London, 1982.

March 1982: I flew up to Glasgow and into deep winter to photograph the Hillhead by-election, where Roy Jenkins was standing (successfully as it turned out) as the candidate of the new Social and Liberal Democrat Party. I was in the office lift with Ian Jack, our reporter, when another journalist got in and said, 'Have you heard? Harry Evans has been sacked.' He had lasted under Murdoch for only a year.

That same month I photographed Sting, born Gordon Sumner, of the rock group Police.

Sting at the recording studio in St John's Wood, London, March 1982.

'Do you believe in God?' asked John Mortimer during his interview with the Archbishop of Canterbury, Dr Robert Runcie, at Lambeth Palace. Mortimer first established that Runcie thought that God was a personal God and then went on to ask why God, if he was omnipotent, allowed the murder of six million Jews. Runcie replied that he was agnostic about that but believed that no human tragedy could not be redeemed in Christ. Mortimer then said, 'But what does being redeemed in Christ mean if you're about to be gassed?'

John Mortimer and Archbishop Robert Runcie at Lambeth Palace, 1982.

June 1982: I collected Peggy from Soho to stay the weekend with us at our house in Long Ditton. She was delighted to ride pillion under the Richmond Park oaks on a superb summer evening. This was a happy time. We were living off an overdraft. We had a splendid house. I rushed around doing my work on a BMW bike. Elizabeth worked occasionally (but would have liked to work much more). The children were wonderful. Elizabeth's Adam and Noah came to see us, and Sarah and Sam were still living with us, Tasha came to stay with us in the holidays. Our house went up in value. And yet we were so busy we hardly noticed the happiness.

Peggy on the BMW RS100 RS, Richmond Park, June 1982.

September 1982: Berlei, the underwear firm, had just been bought for £2 million and I was sent by Business News to do a picture of . . . something. I came back with this one, but the reaction was 'a bit strong, old boy' and it was never used.

Managing Director Bryn Harris of Berlei Ltd, London, 1982.

September 1982: I went with the writer Marjorie Wallace to Grimsby to see Elaine Dale, who has a daughter and son aged four and two. She tended to their needs like any other mother, except that she only used her legs and feet. She didn't have any arms. While we were talking with her, she sat on a table doing the ironing with her feet. Twenty-two years before, her mother took a sedative called Thalidomide to help her during her pregnancy. Along with 451 other children, Elaine Dale received rightful compensation as a result of the *Sunday Times*'s campaign on their behalf.

Elaine Dale with her daughter, Sara, Grimsby, 1982.

November 1982: A rather unhappy meeting with my old friend Joan Collins at a house in Little Venice, where the last days of her third marriage were being endured. I went with the writer Philip Norman. While I was photographing Joan we indulged in friendly chat and, without thinking, I said, 'Seen anything of Max?' Max was her first husband.

She replied, 'He died in 1974.'

'Sorry – I had no idea. How?'

'Cancer.'

'Poor sod.'

I was concentrating on trying to get a good picture, so I wasn't really listening to her reply.

'He deserved it, the bastard,' was what Philip Norman later alleged she had said.

'I really don't know – I didn't hear what she was saying,' I said to Philip, who asked for confirmation in the street afterwards.

The conversation was printed anyway. I had a letter from an angry Joan, who wanted an apology. I wrote back explaining to her that, as a photographer, I had nothing to do with the words that went into the paper and asked her to have lunch with me. There was no reply and I assumed that our friendship, however slight it had been, was now over.

Joan Collins at home in Little Venice, London, 1982.

November 1982: Alfred Brendel was giving a recital in the Queen Elizabeth Hall. I arrived to take pictures of the rehearsal, to find him and Robert Glazebrook, Steinway's general manager, totally absorbed in 'voicing' the piano – the equalization of volume from lowest bass note to top treble. This is done by isolating the strings from one another, so discovering which part of the hammer is causing what result and altering it, or not, by pricking the head of the hammer to make it harder or softer.

It was a fascinating morning. They hardly knew I was there. Every now and then, to test his work, Brendel played a passage from a Beethoven sonata.

Alfred Brendel and Robert Glazebrook 'voicing' the piano, Queen Elizabeth Hall, London, November 1982.

Just before Christmas I went to Stratford East to photograph a black poet called Benjamin Zephaniah. He was so simpatico I could have spent the whole day with him. Many years later, in 2004, he rejected an OBE, saying, 'OBE, me? Up yours.'

Benjamin Zephaniah, poet, Stratford East, London, 1982.

February 1983: My mother, Peggy, had been staying with us and after I drove her back to Soho I carried on north to Hampstead to see Betty, my stepmother. The same musty smell of old clothes and mothballs. For some reason, Betty was dressed in a pair of black knickers and a white silk blouse. She was moving things about in Ronnie's old bedroom. I offered to help her.

As we were moving the bed she said, 'Do you know what attracted me most about your father?'

'No,' I said, only a little curious.

'He had a big cock.'

'Ah,' I said. 'Well now – so that's how it all happened,' and changed the subject as smoothly as possible and left as quickly as possible.

But before I left she gave me some things of Ronnie's, including a photograph of him with John Gielgud in the play *Dear Brutus* and a copy of *The Sunday Referee* from 1936.

Also that month I photographed Tina Brown, who'd just become editor of the *Tatler*. Eight or nine years before she was writing pieces for the *Sunday Times*, which is how she met Harry Evans and became Mrs Evans.

Tina Brown in her office at the Tatler, London, 1983.

Gerald Scarfe — amazing caricaturist — very friendly — photographed his wife, Jane Asher, when she was seventeen. Walks down a different avenue from me — never knew him well — wish I did. Today he was caricaturing Ronald Reagan at his home in Cheyne Walk, Chelsea.

Gerald Scarfe and Ronald Reagan, Chelsea, March 1983.

I first met Germaine Greer in her house in a London square. She opened the door and my first thought was 'what a lovely face'. Then, after she turned and bent over to pick up her post from the floor, my second thought was 'what a lovely bum'. It may have been her reputation for sexual liberation that prompted the thought, but it passed. We were going to visit a convent and when we got there the nuns seem to know her and she them — as though the all-girl Catholic school where she spent her formative years was here in England and not Australia.

Germaine Greer at La Sainte Union, Highgate, March 1983.

'To Michael, with gratitude for turning an ordeal into a pleasure': so Frances Partridge inscribed her book, *Julia – A Portrait of Julia Strachey, by herself and Frances Partridge*. And it was a pleasure: to turn off from Knightsbridge and the 1980s to a quiet house which breathed the 1920s and 1930s, and listen there to this charming woman describe the lives of individuals who wanted to be what they wanted to be to each other, and only hoping to persuade others to their way of thinking.

She was eighty-three when I photographed her and during our afternoon together, over tea, she told me that on the whole her life had been a happy one, though now it seemed to her a little interminable. The following twenty years were filled with a vivacious interest in music, literature and friends. She was 103 when she died.

Frances Partridge, London, May 1983.

Dorchester Hotel, London. Agnetha Fältskog, so wrote Henry Porter in the Atticus column, was once voted to have the most shapely bottom in Europe. Fältskog was part of the Swedish pop group Abba. Porter said I spent more than fifteen minutes circling her to see if the popular vote was justified, and if the object of it might be depicted. I have never understood why she made it so difficult for me. Time compelled me to give up. She also had a great face.

Agnetha Fältskog of Abba, London, May 1983.

12 June 1983: I took Peggy with me to Oxford on a job today. She waited in a café for a couple of hours while I went on the River Cherwell with Henry Porter, who was doing a story for Atticus about punting. We rounded a bend and there were two naked Oxford men, possibly dons, on a stretch of the bank reserved for naked male bathing and known as Parson's Pleasure. 'Sexist Poseurs' reads the graffiti on the screen which shelters them, close to a smaller and more official notice reading 'Ladies Not Permitted Beyond This Point'.

On the Cherwell, Oxford, 1983.

August 1983: I went to New York to be with Elizabeth, who was playing in *The Corn is Green* with Cicely Tyson. After the show one night we got a cab to East 13th Street to hear Count Basie give his eightieth birthday performance. He couldn't walk and had to be helped from his electric wheelchair. The room was full of people near to tears and yet happily aroused to cheers by his playing. He and blues singer Joe Williams blew out the eighty candles on his cake.

Count Basie's eightieth birthday, First City, New York, August 1983.

October 1983: Andrew Neil replaced Frank Giles as editor of the *Sunday Times*. He called the photographers into his office for a meeting – a pep talk, I suppose – in which he gave the impression that he wanted as much good photography in the paper as Harry Evans ever did. We should not have been impressed.

December 1983: She was seven when I first met her, or so the actress Adrienne Corri told me when I went to photograph her. Now she was fifty-two and as beautiful as ever. Oddly, she kept going on about how earlier that week she'd told Sean Connery to fuck off, because he would not stop talking about money. My reason for being with her was that she believed she had found a picture of David Garrick by Gainsborough in a corridor of the Alexandra Theatre in Birmingham. She published a book about her discoveries the next year.

Adrienne Corri, London, 1983.

April 1984: I had the privilege of photographing Richard Branson in his bath on his houseboat in Little Venice.

'What would you like me to do?' he said.

'In an ideal world I would like you reading the *Financial Times* in the bath.'

'Right,' he said. 'No problem.'

When I saw the contacts, I thought it hadn't been such a good idea – there is posing and posing – though the furry cover on the lavatory seat now lends the picture historical interest.

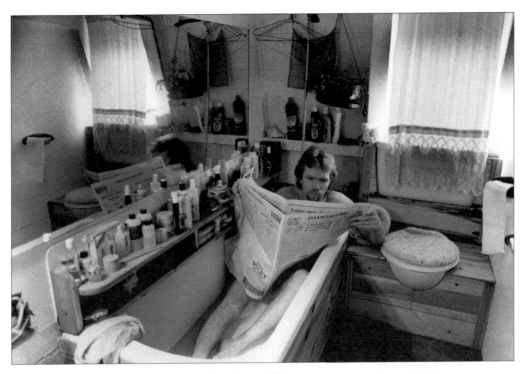

Richard Branson on his boat at Little Venice, 1984.

August 1984: I saw myself for fifteen seconds on TV in *Three Men and a Boat*.

September 1984: I saw myself for two seconds on TV, this time wearing a radio mask and goggles and playing a rear gunner in *The Dam Busters*.

The All England Croquet Championships at the Hurlingham Club, September 1984.

October 1984: Norman Mailer's new novel, *Tough Guys Don't Dance*, was being published and I went with Henry Porter to meet the author at Brown's Hotel in Mayfair. The light was bad, bounced by trim little table lamps, and I felt totally unprepared to cope with what I thought was going to be a tough-talking American, impatient with the vagaries of a middle-aged Englishman. I was quite wrong. He was gentle and almost benign. Later I took him some photographs and asked him to sign one.

Norman Mailer at Brown's Hotel, London, October 1984.

Her Italian father was a painter, her English mother a dancer. When they moved to Australia, she got a job as a cowgirl. Later she trained as an actress at the Old Vic and in 1982 made her first film, for which she had to learn German, *Das Zweite Gesicht* (*The Second Face*). She has a lovely face and this, the last shot of our session, was the closest to the magic I knew was there. Her name is Greta Scacchi.

Greta Scacchi, London, October 1984.

Judi Dench and director Howard Davies during rehearsals of Brecht's *Mother Courage* at the Barbican Theatre, London, October, 1984.

January 1985: Elizabeth and I talked about the problem of my not wanting to make love as often as she would have liked. I didn't like to talk about it because I didn't know the answer. I was constantly having to drive long distances and frequently was not home till after midnight. Being tired was certainly the simplest answer. We had been together for fifteen years and I still loved her, still found her sexually attractive, and I'd have been devastated at any suggestion of parting. Then I thought that I hadn't told a living soul about what had happened with Peggy forty years before and maybe I should tell Elizabeth. Maybe, maybe. When I finally told her, she was angry but not shocked. She told me that she thought what had happened was entirely Peggy's fault and that she was going to put it at the back of her mind. I was very relieved and thankful that she didn't want to leave me. I shall never know if Peggy had damaged me emotionally to the extent that I was unable to respond properly to a loving relationship.

February 1985: After fifty years in a flat behind the Globe and Queen's theatres in Winnett Street, Soho, Peggy moved round the corner to a council flat in Berwick Street. From dilapidated Victoriana to modern tower block, with a lift, constant hot water and central heating. Two rooms, kitchen and bathroom. And still in Soho! Peggy was over the moon, sun and stars.

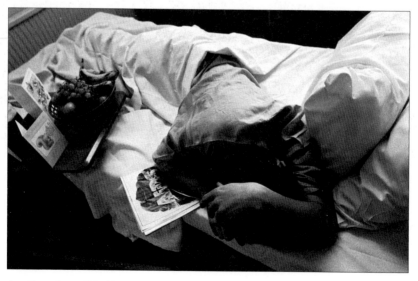

A sufferer from Aids, St Mary's Hospital, Paddington, London, February 1985.

Elizabeth met Francis Bacon in 1956 at a party in Chelsea when she was appearing in *The Pajama Game*. She had dinner with him several times and found him attractive but 'a perfect gentleman' with no inclination to take things further. He was forty-seven and she was twenty-three and unaware that he was gay.

Francis Bacon in front of the left panel of his *Triptych* (1983) at his Tate Gallery show, May 1985.

July 1985: With Oliver Gillie, the medical correspondent, I was summoned to Harefield Hospital, where the surgeon Magda Yacoub was about to transplant a heart and lung – we'd been standing by to photograph such an operation. The patient who was having the transplant was a frail young woman, Debbie Leonard. The operation took nearly five hours and as it proceeded my five cameras got heavier and heavier. There was a strange smell of salty blood. I drove home exhausted at about five in the morning.

Two days later I went back to the hospital and found her sitting by her bed with her mother. She now had a future. A year later, when I went to see her again, she was doing wonderfully well – so well that she had married and had a baby. Then a few years later she died.

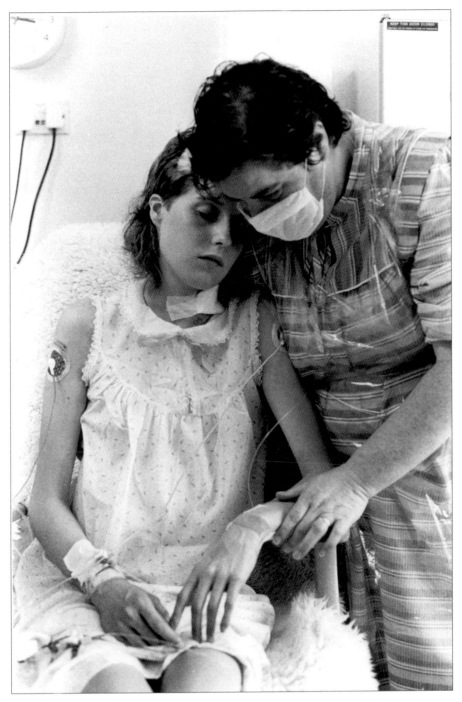

Debbie Leonard, forty-eight hours after her heart and lung transplant at Harefield Hospital, Middlesex, July 1985.

Joseph Beuys, London, October 1985.

October 1985: Joseph Beuys, sculptor and performance artist, had an exhibition at the Anthony D'Offay Gallery near Bond Street. The exhibition comprised rolls and rolls of carpet felt laid around the gallery with, in the middle, a black grand piano. The piano was closed and locked and had a music stand and a thermometer on top.

Beuys crashed in the frozen wastes of the Crimea while flying for the Luftwaffe in the Second World War. His rescuers, nomad Tartars, kept him warm by wrapping him in felt. He wore his hat constantly, probably to hide head injuries sustained in the crash. The diamond-hard silence of his seemingly defensive disposition was broken occasionally by the gentleness of his voice. He died two months later at the age of sixty-five.

I went to photograph Dame Peggy Ashcroft on location in a beautiful eighteenth-century house in Hitchin. She was starring in a TV play about Agatha Christie called *Murder by the Book*. When I was angling for a shot between takes, she looked at me coldly and crossly.

Peggy Ashcroft as Agatha Christie, Hitchin, England, October 1985.

January 1986: Rupert Murdoch moved his newspapers to a new and non-unionized print plant at Wapping. The printing unions refused to go, which was probably what Murdoch wanted: another print staff had been trained and were already in place. Many journalists were undecided. To go or not to go? I felt with many others that I didn't have much choice – I had a mortgage and what seemed a secure job, and in any case the stubborn behaviour of the print unions had won them few friends on the editorial floors. At a National Union of Journalists meeting the staff voted to go, sixty-eight votes for and sixty-two against. On 28 January I went to Wapping, to the refurbished rum warehouses that were the new offices of the *Sunday Times*. The print unions picketed the plant for many months and the number of demonstrators reached into the thousands. It was like working inside a besieged fortress, protected by barbed wire and the Metropolitan Police.

By the spring the unions had not given up the siege. Wapping from the inside, 1986.

November 1986: The pickets are still screaming 'scab' at us every time we go into Wapping or leave it. A relief to be at King's College, Cambridge, to watch Ismail Merchant and James Ivory making a film of E. M. Forster's novel *Maurice*. It was pissing down with rain, so they couldn't work outside. I found myself in an undergraduate's room so small I wasn't allowed to take photographs until they broke for lunch; then I was allowed five minutes. A young actor called Hugh Grant was in the cast.

Later that month doctors found an extreme swelling of Peggy's aorta and gave her from three months to three years to live.

Hugh Grant and the director James Ivory on location at King's College, Cambridge, November 1986.

1 January 1987: Elizabeth, Peggy and I had a New Year's breakfast together. We had a grimly humorous conversation about death. Peggy said, 'When I die I don't want a funeral. In the flip-up part of my desk you'll find the papers giving my body for medical research. You can have the body back after three years.' Well, thanks! said Elizabeth and I. To which Peggy replied, 'Well, after they've finished with me you can bury the bones – though what for I can't imagine.' We laughed, as we had to. Later in the morning I found Peggy sitting by the window in tears. She wanted to have an operation on her aorta, but the surgeon said she had a very poor chance of surviving it. She will soon be eighty.

After walking the dogs in the rain, we drove to Hampstead with a double-bed mattress in the back of the car to see Fay, my third wife. She has no job and no money and lives off public support. We struggled with the mattress up four floors. Elizabeth did some hoovering. On the way home, Elizabeth said that Fay's orange juice was laced with gin.

Lucy Lambton, the Rectory, Hedgerley, February 1987.

February 1987: To Hedgerley — a delightful village, second exit off the M40. Here I met the engagingly eccentric author and photographer Lucy Lambton, who, after I had mistakenly spoken to her as the missing Lord Lucan's daughter, turned out to be the child of the less (but still faintly) notorious Lord Lambton. She was living in a beautiful big eighteenth-century rectory, which she said she liked so much that she refused to live in the house of the man she'd recently married, Peregrine Worsthorne, the newspaper editor and writer. She said they spent weekends together. She didn't say which house.

July 1987: A flight to Dublin and then a hire car for an hour's drive to County Wicklow to see John Boorman, the film director. I arrived as they were finishing lunch, but his wife brought me some apple and blackberry pie and invited me to sit at the table, around which were gathered his two lovely daughters, a priest and a journalist. I had my Leica round my neck and took this picture without asking if I might. Boorman seemed a little annoyed. I was there because he was directing a semi-autobiographical film about his life in London during the Blitz called *Hope and Glory*.

John Boorman, County Wicklow, July 1987.

October 1987: My life as a newspaper photographer seems increasingly mean-ingless – the routine of taking pictures that do no more than add a little visual interest to a story, taken quickly, and cropped or rejected even more quickly. I'm usually happier at the piano, or French-polishing tables, or restoring sash windows. But sometimes, even now, it has its rewards.

The Fine Arts Society in Bond Street celebrated the eightieth birthday of Helen Lessore with an exhibition of her paintings. She was married to portrait sculptor Frederick Lessore and in 1923 they founded the Beaux Arts Gallery to promote avante-garde art in England. When we met she was very wary of me, and chided me that there was very little in the world to be happy about and that her friends would not understand if there was a smiling photograph of her in the paper. I later learned that she liked the photo that was used. She died in 1994.

Helen Lessore at her eightieth birthday exhibition of her paintings, London, October 1987.

Ashley Page started his professional career with the Royal Ballet and went on to become a leading member of the company. He continued as a choreographer, unyielding in his demands for modernity in dance. I photographed a moment from a new ballet of his, *The Angel of Death is in My Bed Tonight*, in the basement at the Royal Ballet's headquarters in Covent Garden.

The Angel of Death is in My Bed Tonight, a ballet by Ashley Page, October 1987.

February 1988: Today I was asked to photograph a junior fashion show – three-and four-year olds showing what designers thought the Duchess of York's baby might wear! I was halfway through the afternoon, doing the most dull photographs, when Mike Cranmer, our picture editor, bleeped me. 'Would I buy some spring flowers and use a little flash? It's for the front page.' I nearly quit. When he saw the pictures, he said three times, 'Well done, Mike.' I don't think I've ever been so depressed about a picture used on the front – as though the *Sunday Times* were a broadsheet *Sun*. There was no story and the pictures were banal. I whispered to Peter Dunne, my old friend and photographer colleague, who was doing a stint on the desk, that I hated the pictures everybody was so pleased about. To cheer me up he said, 'My dear fellow, it's what they want. Perfect! It'll look very good.'

'Varnishing Day' at the Royal Academy summer exhibition, May 1988. The big picture is Gillian Ayres's *Here We Come a-Piping*.

There was a lovely moment at the Royal Opera House while I was photographing Sir Frederic Ashton rehearsing a revival of his last full-length ballet, *Ondine*, with Anthony Dowell and Maria Almeida. Ashton was going through some positions when he suddenly kissed both their hands as though thanking them for their work. I took a picture, but fearful that I had missed it I asked him to repeat the kiss. This, the first one I took, was the best; the others showed their self-consciousness.

Frederic Ashton, Anthony Dowell and Maria Almeida at the Royal Opera House, May 1988.

Allen Jones's life-size sculptures of extremely sexy women posing as furniture were both admired and censured. When I met him at the Waddington Galleries, London, his slender appearance and unassuming manner misled me into thinking he was the opposite of what he was — a champion heavyweight in his own ring.

Allen Jones with his sculpture *Sprawl* at the Waddington Galleries, London, August 1988.

February 1989: Another monumental with Elizabeth. I reached a new low in my behaviour. I spat at her. I was so ashamed – it put me into a shocked state. I was trying not to be violent to her and on the instant thought that spitting wouldn't hurt her but would relieve my frustration. She in no way deserved such a horrible thing. I told her how sorry and ashamed I was. Later she said she thought this was the end of our marriage, but she was so forgiving.

October 1989: To the Haymarket to photograph *A Life in the Theatre* for which I was awarded the BP Arts Journalism Award FPR 1989 – Denholm Elliott playing on old actor. A lot of people seemed to like this picture and I think the reason was they thought I had taken a rather clever shot in Elliott's dressing room. But it was taken from the stalls. Elliott wasn't looking into a mirror but through a frame. He died of an Aids-related disease at his home in Ibiza in 1992.

Denholm Elliott in *A Life in the Theatre* at the Haymarket Theatre, London, October 1989.

16 February 1990: My mother, Peggy, was admitted suddenly to University College Hospital in Gower Street. When I got there the registrar told me that Peggy's aorta had burst and that she would die in a few hours. I was taken to see her. She was lying on a trolley wearing an oxygen mask, which made it very difficult for us to talk. A nurse took the mask off for us and we began chatting. She wasn't feeling too bad and we laughed and joked a bit, with her telling me she had had to go to the loo in the washing-up basin. A little later she was moved to a ward on the first floor. After a while, she seemed comfortable and I told her I was going to fetch some night things for her as she might have to stay in hospital for a few days.

When I got back, they'd drawn the curtains round her bed. She started having a bad pain in her chest and back. 'Why do I have to go through this? I don't deserve it.' I asked the nurse if there was something she could give her to ease the pain. There was a lot of toing and froing with the doctor, but eventually she was given another morphine injection. I held Peggy's hand and the nurse held mine as we tried to comfort her, but the pain seemed to be getting worse. I looked at the nurse and asked what we could do. She said, 'I can put up the dosage a bit.' I said, 'If we can — we must. We have to stop this pain.' She put up the dosage. I hugged and kissed Peggy, trying to help her through the pain. It started to ease and she smiled at me and said, 'It's been an honour to know you.' I squeezed her hand and smiled feebly, trying to hold back my tears. Her breathing was getting very weak, but she smiled as I took a picture of her. Then her eyes found me and she said, 'This is it.' I made some absurd remark about her being fit to go home in a few days. But she was right. A few minutes later I couldn't make out if she was breathing. I asked the nurse if she had gone and she checked her pulse and said, 'Yes.'

An unsuitably ludicrous scene then occurred. Peggy had died with her mouth open and I asked the nurse to close her mouth for me to take a picture of her. She tried to close it several times, but it wouldn't stay closed. So I took a few just as she was: her lines smooth, her face fast asleep. Earlier she had said she was going to have a ball seeing her friends and family again after so long. I so hoped she was right.

Her body went to the University College Hospital.

18 March 1990: We had a wake for Peggy. People started to arrive at 10.30 on a perfect sunny morning at our village hall in West End, Esher. We brought the food, drinks, flowers and extra chairs over from the cottage. About 100 of her friends and two of my ex-wives, Susan and Fay, were there. A tape recorder played Benny Goodman and Artie Shaw. I almost broke down saying a few words. My friend and *Sunday Times* colleague Bryan Wharton fired fourteen shots from a blank pistol to commemorate her birth date – 14 February 1907. The reception to this paramilitary salute was mixed, but it was marvellous of him to have thought of it. The last guest left at 11.30 and by midnight we had cleared all the tables and chairs, cleaned the hall, and put the key back through a letter box on the other side of the common.

Peggy at University College Hospital, 16 February 1990,
shortly before and shortly after she died.

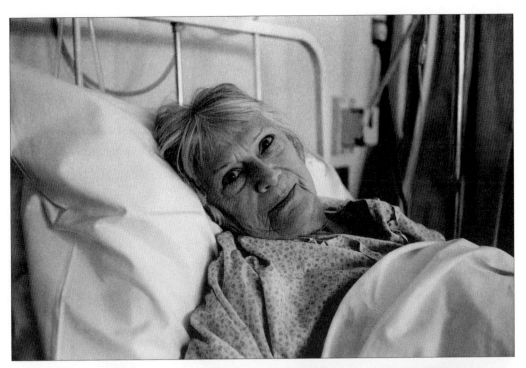

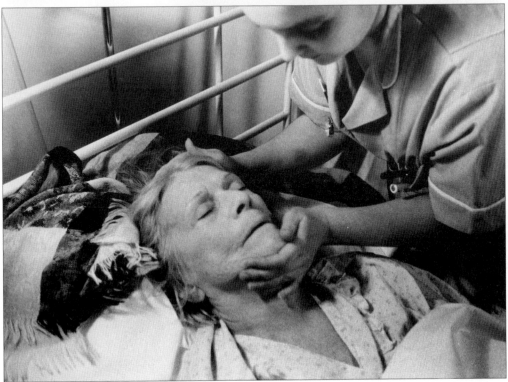

March 1991: The great boogie-woogie pianist Fats Domino was playing at the Albert Hall and the last thing he needed was publicity; the house was packed and photographers were allowed in only after the concert started, when we were given a grudging ten minutes to take our pictures from a sitting or lying position in one of the aisles. The only thing in our favour was plenty of light. I lay on my stomach, with acute pain in my elbows, trying to get a close-up of the extraordinary silver ring and cufflinks that Fats Domino was wearing while at the same time including a recognizable part of his face. After several failures, I managed to get this shot.

Fats Domino at the Albert Hall, March 1990.

340

October 1991: Soft, intimidating opulence of the Savoy Hotel. I was there to photograph Arthur Miller, the American playwright, in London for the opening of his play, *The Ride Down Mt Morgan* at Wyndham's Theatre. At the end of a long, silent corridor the man who had been married to Marilyn Monroe led me into his riverside suite. He had large glasses and big hands. A ready smile accompanied his deep, soft American speech. In spite of his reputation he appeared as nervous as I was as he told me that he hoped that the reviews would be good. The conversation was slowing down a bit and I realized he had had enough. I shot as quickly as possible, hoping the magic moment would come before I had to leave. The magic came just before my time ran out.

Arthur Miller at the Savoy Hotel, London, October 1991.

January 1991: My eldest daughter, Sam, got married. And what a performance! There were two weddings, a civil and a religious, at a town hall in France and the Russian Orthodox Church in Geneva. At the first, Sam arrived looking like a pre-war Hollywood film star, with bright red lips and a set hairdo, and glitteringly happy. Elizabeth was very happy because two of her children, Noah and Adam, were there.

Wedding morning: my younger daughter, Tasha, Natalia (Tasha and Sam's grandmother), Sam and Lisa (her mother and my fourth wife), January 1991.

A year later Sam made me a grandfather for the first time with a beautiful girl, Charlie. She and her husband, Cedric, had two more children, Tom and Felix, and then their marriage fell apart. In 1997 my other daughter, Tasha, and her husband, Cara, produced a lovely girl, Leah. Their relationship fell apart eight years later, three months after they were married. In 2004, another girl, Irina, was fathered by David, her present partner. Both my daughters live in Paris, where Sam works for Louis Vuitton, and Tasha served an apprenticeship with Henri Cartier-Bresson's printers. When the 92-year-old Cartier Bresson visited to check the prints of his retrospective exhibition, her smile persuaded him to allow her to photograph him. After the eighth shot, he said, 'No more,' and she finished with a shot of him pretending to shoot her with his walking stick.

Tasha pregnant with Leah, December 1996.

Cartier-Bresson at his printers, Paris 2002.

I retired from the *Sunday Times* in 1994. The paper, for all its faults and frustrations in the later years, had been good to me. I have been lucky to meet the people I did — until the end, I was photographing artists of the calibre of Pavarotti, Rostropovich, Menuhin, Arthur Miller. But lucky though these meetings were, they were not my main luck, the luck of my life, which was to meet and marry Elizabeth. Her children, Adam and Noah, are successfully married and living in America, as is Sarah in Paris. They and their families accept me and my shortcomings with great affection. In 1997 we sold our cottage in Esher and moved to a small house above the Brede valley near Rye in East Sussex. As I write this I am seventy-seven, with many of the expected problems of age in attendance — a heart rescued by a triple bypass, bad legs, wheezing chest — all of them kept in some kind of running order by a variety of pills.

There is a noticeable return of my childhood's whims and fancies, and my mind still wanders to places where, fortunately, my body fears to tread. The sexual drawbacks of age have simplified our relationship into a passionate friendship. Elizabeth is seventy-two, pretty and well, with remarkably little deterioration in a figure that still shows what a dancer she was and is, and her face still shines at you, though this will always be my favourite picture of her.

Elizabeth through the window, 1972.

Index

Figures in italics indicate captions.

351

355